JOURNEYING
· BETWEEN THE ·
WORLDS

About the Author

Eagle Skyfire is a respected elder and spiritual teacher with over thirty years' experience in helping people find their life purpose and meaningful growth in their personal spiritual journeys while sharing the traditions she has learned from various Native American spiritual teachers. Her hands-on, practical approach is successful in assisting countless people in a wide range of ways, such as developing their intuitive and shamanic skills, creating personal spiritual practices, understanding past lives and soul work. Many people from around the world seek her for readings on personal and professional matters, connecting with loved ones who have crossed over, communicating with animals, and interpreting dreams and visions.

Over the years she has been asked to share her knowledge at various community and professional events as a cultural and spiritual presenter. Eagle Skyfire has guided many people to manifest healthier and whole lives.

On her website, www.eagleskyfire.com, she has a popular blog called *Flow of the River*, where she shares what she interprets from the sacred flow of energy around us. Many people look forward to this guidance on a weekly basis. She also directs a live local radio talk show on WCHE 1520 AM called *Fresh Perspective*, in which she provides an overview of the Flow of the River and welcomes callers every Monday.

JOURNEYING
• BETWEEN THE •
WORLDS

Walking with the Sacred Spirits
Through Native American
Shamanic Teachings & Practices

EAGLE SKYFIRE

Llewellyn Publications
Woodbury, Minnesota

FIRST EDITION
Fourth Printing, 2024

Cover design by Shannon McKuhen
Interior design by Lauryn Heineman
Interior illustrations by Wen Hsu

Llewellyn Publications is a registered trademark of Llewellyn Worldwide Ltd.

Library of Congress Cataloging-in-Publication Data
    Names: Skyfire, Eagle, author.
    Title: Journeying between the worlds : walking with the sacred spirits
        through Native American Shamanic teachings & practices / Eagle Skyfire.
    Description: First Edition. | Woodbury : Llewellyn Worldwide, Ltd., 2019.
    Identifiers: LCCN 2018060958 (print) | LCCN 2019017550 (ebook) | ISBN
        9780738760711 (ebook) | ISBN 9780738760346 (alk. paper)
    Subjects: LCSH: Indians of North America—Religion. | Spiritual
        healing--Shamanism. | Shamanism.
    Classification: LCC E98.R3 (ebook) | LCC E98.R3 S49 2019 (print) | DDC
        299.7/138—dc23
    LC record available at https://lccn.loc.gov/2018060958

Llewellyn Worldwide Ltd. does not participate in, endorse, or have any authority or responsibility concerning private business transactions between our authors and the public.

All mail addressed to the author is forwarded but the publisher cannot, unless specifically instructed by the author, give out an address or phone number.

Any internet references contained in this work are current at publication time, but the publisher cannot guarantee that a specific location will continue to be maintained. Please refer to the publisher's website for links to authors' websites and other sources.

Llewellyn Publications
A Division of Llewellyn Worldwide Ltd.
2143 Wooddale Drive
Woodbury, MN 55125-2989
www.llewellyn.com

Printed in the United States of America

Acknowledgments

It is with the deepest gratitude in my Heart that I would like to give my thanks to the Great Spirit for being given the gift of my lessons and this beautiful life. To my patron, Lord Feathered Serpent, who guides me unerringly and shows me how to evolve. To All My Relations seen and unseen, without your steadfast love and assistance, I would not be where I am today. To all my Medicine Teachers from various tribes and nations, I thank you for your love, patience, and faith in me as you taught me the ways of the Good Red Road. In particular I would like to acknowledge with much love my Uncle Bear and Auntie Brenda, who have unfailingly guided me and helped me to grow over the years. A special thank-you to Reverend Carl Letson, who gave me encouragement and confirmed the lessons of the Medicine Wheel and some of the current opinions of the Native American community that I share in this book. I would also like to extend my gratitude to my true friends and true family who put up with me on a regular basis and have given me their ideas for use in this book. To Laura, my daughter, who is the joy of my life and always encourages me. To Donna, who always believed in me and who has been my Sherpa in this twenty-first century. I give thanks to my students, who are some of my greatest teachers. Without your suggestions this book would not be as thorough as it is.

And last, to you, dear reader, I am grateful for your willingness to share your time with me as you study my culture and traditions to guide you on your spiritual journey. All of you are such a blessing in my life! May the Great Spirit abundantly bless you with the gifts of health, happiness, and help.

Disclaimer

Although this ancient tradition can give you deep insights, it is never meant to replace professional help. Always consult a physician, therapist, or other professional for your specific needs. Shamanism is meant to be a complementary modality to support these mainstream methods.

It is my honor to share these teachings with you, and they are meant to empower you. However, completing them does not make you a shaman nor adopt you officially into any tribe. In truth, there many within the Native American community who hold the opinion that the term *shaman* is a misnomer of their spiritual teachers and healers; however, this feeling is not unanimous.

This book barely scratches the surface of what is required to become a spiritual healer. Becoming a sanctioned traditional spiritual healer of a nation that you belong to takes many years of constant training under the careful guidance of a spiritual leader and tribal elders. What exists here is a resource for you to make use of in your own personal practice. Trying to perform any of the exercises or techniques that I am giving you here for other people may cause great harm to you and to them. Please use these techniques for your own well-being only; do not attempt them for anyone else.

Contents

Exercises and Journeys

Chapter 9

Introduction

I have been walking between the worlds all my life and as a child displayed strong spiritual and shamanic abilities. I was misunderstood and often felt caught between the world of spirits and humankind. It was very hard, as I did not know where I fit in, if anywhere at all. It was on the Good Red Road that I found out who I am and what I am.

While I was born into a multigenerational South American Indigenous tradition, it's not something that I was formally taught as part of my regular upbringing because it was thought to be unnecessary in this modern age. Eventually, though, my natural inclination toward these sacred practices led me to be adopted by a powerful spirit man, Ted Silverhand, who is of the Tuscarora Nation, Bear clan, into the traditions he follows. It has been both a blessing and a challenge to live in this mainstream society while learning the old ways, and so it has given me valuable insight on how to relay these teachings in a way that is meaningful to those from mainstream culture.

I am privileged to have learned from Native American teachers from many nations throughout my life. When I was very young, about eight to ten years old, I was taught the ways of the Tuscarora. As I grew, I was granted permission to receive teachings from the Seneca, Anishinaabe, and Cherokee, and a little from the Lakota Nations. As the years passed, I continued my walk through the Americas and received wisdom from the Taino, Inca, and Maya. I was granted permission to share some of the wisdom from each of my Medicine Teachers. I write to the universal Heart of the Good Red Road to respect the individual tribes, for only they can determine with whom to share their unique ceremonies.

My experiences afford me a unique view of the commonalities of Native American spirituality and the uniqueness of the culture that each tribe holds. It also has allowed me a "one away" perspective from mainstream society. Early on, it was challenging at times to translate and to convey teachings from the old ways into this culture that has no point of reference. However, after teaching for so many years, it is now my honor not only to act as a living bridge between this world and that of the spirits, but also to relay some of the timeless wisdom of the First People while walking in twenty-first-century mainstream society. I aspire to impart the ancient teachings of this land in a sacred way that honors what the Great Spirit has given to us yet remains relevant to the peoples of today.

I have been sharing Native American traditions and spirituality for several decades. I realized that although there are several good books on shamanism, none of them offered simple step-by-step exercises for a beginner who wished to integrate Native

American spirituality into their daily spiritual practices. I offer this book as a guide for those who wish to learn this ancient art in a practical and structured way. The lessons offered here are teachings from my teachers from the several nations that have given me permission to share their wisdom. I do this because I wish to honor all my teachers. This book is meant to help people grow in their private shamanic practices and connect with their personal protectors and the land in a sacred way. It is my hope that what I share here will guide non–Native American people to be respectful of the old ways and First People of this land and will encourage Native American people who are seeking their heritage to return to their roots.

I have written this book in the style I teach. I like a "hands-on" approach and I know many people prefer to learn that way. Because of this, I share exercises after each important teaching. Each exercise is designed to immerse you in the experience and ingrain the lesson. They will help you discern what is an actual spiritual experience or a message from the spirit realms versus your mental chatter or emotional desires. But in order for you to truly understand the lessons in the coming chapters, you must open more than just your mind. You must open your Heart. I am not asking you to change your beliefs, but I offer these teachings to you as a sharing of and an exposure to Native American traditions and culture.

At times you will notice certain words being capitalized that normally are not. This is done to show respect to aspects within ourselves and to entities that are divine, much like you would capitalize a proper noun.

This book is written for beginners who want to learn how to safely practice a form of traditional Native American spirituality and develop practices that help them grow stronger in their connection to nature, to their inner knowing, and to sacred helping spirits. It is meant to be followed in the order it was written. Each exercise is a stepping-stone to the next foundational exercise, culminating in you being able to journey with confidence and begin to interpret the messages that are given to you. You will have the greatest success if you master the exercises one at a time in the order in which they are presented. As with anything, the amount of dedication you give to learning this ancient discipline, the more comfortable and ultimately proficient you will become.

Realize this is very different from learning how to perform another activity. What you are holding in your hands right now is wisdom from the ages that will open the door to a dynamic, ever-evolving relationship with the Great Spirit, your sacred self, and All Your Relations seen and unseen. This is not to be approached casually, but with the deep respect and concentration due to an aspect of spirituality that has guided and still is so deeply guiding our people throughout time. It is in my Heart for the ancient and timeless to blend with the new so as to heal and guide future generations. *Ah-ho!*

· ONE ·

What Is a Shaman?

A *shaman* is an individual who is chosen by the sacred spirits and their tribal elders to act as an intermediary between the natural and supernatural worlds. They are trained in various rituals to help cure illness, foretell the future, interpret dreams and signs from the spirits, and reinforce harmony between the physical and spiritual worlds. Much like most other abilities, individuals are either born with this predisposition or train very hard to try to obtain some level of skill. But there are certain characteristics common to all shamans regardless of where they hail from.

The first one is the ability to sense and to communicate with nonhuman beings such as animals, plants, and spirits. There is also the natural ability to walk from this three-dimensional reality into alternate forms of reality at will, which is called *journeying*. A shaman has an intrinsic need to be deeply connected to nature, and nature welcomes the shaman. A shaman can't help but see things from a very different perspective. Sometimes it is very difficult for people who are born shamans to fit in, and they're not supposed to. So someone who is born a shaman will most likely have used these abilities before ever being trained.

The difference between a trained and untrained shaman is similar to someone taking lessons to perfect a skill versus someone who doesn't. For example, someone might be a born athlete and play sports well, but without training, it is unlikely they would become a professional or an Olympian.

In truth, every culture throughout the world throughout time has had shamans in it. But for now, I'll keep it simple—I'll classify shamans into two basic categories. Neither form is superior to the other, as each classification has its strengths and weaknesses.

The first type is *neoshamanism*. *Neo-* means "new" in Greek, and this form of shamanism has developed in modern times. It is based on studying different forms of indigenous shamanism from various cultures. Typically, the practices are taken out of their cultural context and stripped down to their minimum elements. The neoshaman has the advantage of being able to borrow and mix and match at will from different cultures and countries from around the globe into one practice. Neoshamanism has tremendous flexibility. The disadvantage is that since neoshamans are not held to any particular spiritual or cultural context, sometimes it can be very difficult for them to decipher who or what is working with them unless they've developed personal relationships with these other beings.

A *traditional shaman* is one who is beholden to a particular tradition and culture. A traditional shaman is expected to learn a code of conduct and in turn pass on the different rites of passage, teaching stories, and techniques that would be necessary to perform healing rites; to interpret messages, dreams, and signs; and to act as an intermediary between the seen and unseen worlds. The disadvantage, however, is that for the most part the traditional shaman, being beholden to a particular culture and tradition, is expected to remain within it and thus cannot borrow from any others. The rites of initiation that are unique to that culture are performed to introduce a shaman to a specific set of sacred beings, or *pantheon*, which creates a formal alliance between them.

Why Is a Traditional Shaman Needed in the Twenty-First Century?

In this book we will be working with traditional shamanism, based on the techniques given to me by my Tuscarora, Seneca, Anishinaabe, and Taino teachers. Although it might seem that there would be no need for traditional shamanic practices outside the reservation or tribal lands, the same problems that plagued all our ancestors, regardless of where we came from, can be found in our society today. I truly believe that crime comes from an individual's inability to connect with their sacred self in addition to the greater disassociation we have from each other in our society. We need to learn how to reconnect with own Hearts, which in turn will help us see that we are truly one family no matter where we come from. Depression, anxiety, and other mental illnesses can be exacerbated by societal factors; it's important to know how to be still and tap into the peace that can be found within. Learning the art of meditation and knowing how to properly connect with your helpers seen and unseen through shamanic practices can help you cope with this.

Children need to be taught about the respect for All That Is. The techniques of building community and finding the Power Within were taught by both the tribal elders and the shaman.

The Sacred Hoop of the generations is broken. It needs to be mended by young people connecting with their elders, which is part of the shamanic tradition. Young people can benefit from the elders' experience and avoid repeating the same mistakes. The young can also see how things have come to be and what are solid foundations to build the future upon. The older generations can benefit from the creativity and fresh perspectives of the younger generation. In this way the Sacred Hoop of Life in the Americas can be mended. Traditional shamans are found all over the world, and they assist in making sure that the Sacred Hoop is preserved and, when needed, restored. Whatever solutions can be found in nature, from the spirits, and from a culture's spiritual teachings are used to help with reconnecting people and their communities with sacred Power so that all may live in beauty, Balance, and harmony. Addressing these global needs is as relevant today as it was centuries ago.

What Does a Traditional Shaman Do?

A shaman is a person who acts as a living bridge between our world and the realm of nature and spirits. Hollywood might have you think that a shaman is typically on a hallucinogenic drug trip most of the time. However, the truth is that tribes that use hallucinogenic drugs were given them as gifts from the gods or sacred nature spirits. The plants themselves are living holy entities that carry powerful energy, and they are only administered as sacraments. An individual is prepared by a shaman or Medicine person before the hallucinogenic plant is given during a ritual. The purpose of this sacrament is to introduce the candidate to the spirit realms and to open the channel within that person to receive divine energy. Using these plants for recreational purposes is disrespectful and sacrilegious.

The trained shaman understands that there is a tremendous responsibility in taking on this position as an emissary between the realms while helping maintain the health of the community they serve. A shaman helps solve the problems of both the individual and the community by making sure that they are both equally supportive of each other. Many shamans are keepers of tradition and help pass on the teaching stories and rituals that will preserve the wellness of their people. From their training, they are able to perform ceremonies of healing. It takes many years to learn about the herbs that can heal the body in addition to other rituals that help cleanse people and places from evil spirits and toxic energies. Yet other ceremonies help realign the community with the cycles of nature, sacred time, and divine energies greater than their own so that harmony can be maintained.

It is also the responsibility of the traditional shaman to carefully choose and initiate the next generation of shamans so that the sacred teachings given to their people won't be lost to the passage of time. This is in addition to helping people find themselves and even more so when they become lost due to a traumatic event. Some shamans are trained to help find children, property, or animals. We also help retrieve more than just people or physical items. We perform healing rituals that retrieve an individual's personal Power and soul. Soul retrieval helps a person's soul be restored. It helps them become reintegrated so they can move forward as a whole and healthy person. Power retrievals help reunite a person or a community with their energy and realign the energy into harmony with All That Is. Power retrieval is a ritual that allows them to properly reclaim and learn how to channel the energy of life that is being gifted back to them.

We also retrieve wisdom of the ancient spirits and can give advice on personal matters. Some of this wisdom is used to help build a better community. The trained shaman can help connect you to your spiritual helpers and assist you in finding your guides in the spirit world. Through much training and study, we develop the ability to interpret dreams and visions so that they may give you insight and clarity to walk more strongly upon your life path. Yet other shamans learn how to guide souls into the afterlife so that the departed and the living may have peace. Overall, a traditional shaman will help the individual awaken to their personal Power and guide them in how to utilize it correctly as they grow into their purpose in life.

Some shamans choose to completely focus on a particular area of expertise. These shamans would be very much like the medical specialists you would see for a more acute physical ailment. Some study to become herbalists. They learn to Walk intimately with the spirits of the plants and trees in addition to learning of their medicinal properties. Others choose to become adept in the healing of the mind and soul. They study hard to learn about how a person's life lessons throughout lifetimes is impacting the present, how the Sacred Cycles of Life interact with each other and guide a person to embrace their nature in a Balanced way instead of working against it. They assist an individual in establishing a sense of inner well-being and understanding how they can participate fully in their lives.

Some shamans choose a riskier line to specialize in. These are shamans who help cleanse people and areas of strong evil forces and demonic beings. It is a very rare type of individual who is willing to put themselves in harm's way. They have to undergo rigorous training that will protect them from being corrupted by the very things that they are trying to save an individual or the community from. Other shamans, like myself, are ritual leaders. We are taught the rituals, teachings, and sacred stories that help preserve our people so they can live in harmony with All Our Relations. Obviously, this is not an exhaustive list of the types of shamans that exist. These, however, are the most common types that you will find throughout the world.

How Are Shamans Chosen?

You may wonder how certain people are chosen to become shamans. Typically, the tribal elders and shaman of a tribe or nation see the potential in an individual. Depending on the customs of the specific nation, the training starts when the candidate is a young child or when they come of age. The person displays the natural abilities and probably has used them unknowingly. At times, you can feel the sacred Power flowing through them. The individual might display their abilities through *Seeing*, the ability to accurately perceive the past (which may include past lives) and future events, through communication with the spirits and animals or through channeling sacred energy for the benefit of all.

However, natural ability and intelligence are not enough. The people who are finally selected by the tribal elders and shaman are those who display respect for life, humility, and purity of Heart. The candidates must show that they have the ability to be compassionate and think beyond themselves with a strong desire to serve their community and Creator while respecting the Balance of all life. Only then are individuals selected to begin the training that usually takes several years. I was made to undergo over a decade of training. For many years, those in training can only perform rituals under the supervision of another ceremonial leader or shaman before they are initiated to be a full-fledged shaman.

How Will You Benefit from Learning Traditional Shamanism?

If you picked up this book, I would bet that you have more than just a mild curiosity about traditional shamanism. You picked up this book because some part of you deep inside felt called to this spiritual practice. You easily connect with nature on a very deep level and more than likely have spoken with spirits and animals more than once at some time during your life. In addition to this, I am sure that there are many of you who are ready to reclaim your sacred self. And so, it is the teachings inside these pages that have called you to it.

There are many ways in which this path will enrich your life. It will help you tap into your own spiritual Power, which we call the *Fire Within*. This will enable you to reconnect with nature and the cycles of nature in a very profound way. You will learn how to be still to listen to the *Voice Within*. It is here within you that the deep Knowing resides, and it will connect you to All That Is. Through this connection, you will find that you will be able to receive universal wisdom and feel inner peace. By accessing your inner wisdom, you will be better able to guide yourself throughout the different areas of your everyday life. You will also be shown how to properly connect to the spirit realms that lie beyond the five physical senses in order to find and interact with the spirits and sacred beings in a safe and proper way. All of this will promote your personal growth, which can lead you to personal transformation. This evolution will help you discover your life purpose. Finally, I feel that one of the greatest benefits is being able to live in greater harmony and Balance. You feel confident and at home no matter where you may be so that you can live to the fullest.

· TWO ·

Basic Native American Spiritual Concepts

Here I will introduce basic spiritual concepts of the First Peoples of the Americas, including the concepts that will help you walk the Good Red Road. Realize please that I'm touching upon universal concepts that are found in some form or interpretation throughout the various tribes of the Americas. From a First Peoples standpoint, all of North America, the islands of the Caribbean and the Virgin Islands, and South America are considered *Native America*. If you wish to learn from a specific tribal nation, I ask that you respectfully approach those elders. They alone have the right to teach you and to initiate you into the specific sacred pathways of their tribe or nation.

While my early training came from the Tuscarora and the Anishinaabe, over the years it spanned to include teachings from the Cherokee, Seneca, Lakota, Taino, and the Maya. I consider what I am sharing traditional Native American shamanism because my teachings are strictly from the First Peoples throughout the Americas only.

The Good Red Road

Native American people do not have a religion but a sacred way of walking through the world. Indigenous spirituality is also known as the *Good Red Road*. The Good Red Road is the Native American term used to describe an individual's unique spiritual walk through life. It is a way of being, one of reverence and compassion for all life, including your own. It is a spiritual pathway that believes that all things are cyclical yet have different expressions each time they return. These cycles are called *Sacred Hoops* and include the turning of the seasons, when the younger and older generations come together, yearly celebrations, or the high and low tides of the ocean, to name a few.

As much as possible when Walking upon this spiritual path, be mindful of completing the Sacred Hoop. This means never taking more than you can give. Make your decisions by taking into account the impact of your actions on both the physical and spiritual worlds, not only for now but potentially for many generations to come. I present to you the modern example of the concept of *precycling*. This is the practice of only buying something if you already know in advance how you are going to responsibly recycle or donate the item when you are done with it, versus just throwing it in the trash and creating more pollution for our planet. I think the practical benefits of this are obvious, but the spiritual benefits are keeping beautiful, healthy, and clean energy in a vibrant environment for future generations. Be mindful that I am speaking not only of human beings but also of the future generations of All Our Relations.

Power: The Breath of the Great Spirit

The essence of the universe is harmony. Because of this, the universe always strives to maintain a state of Balance, much like our bodies strive to do in order to be healthy. The Breath of the Creator is called *Power*. It is a concept found in other cultures. In Hinduism it is known as *prana*; in Taoism it is known as *chi*. In pop culture it is known as *the Force*.

Native American spirituality is an Earthway. An *Earthway* is when an individual *must* connect compassionately with all living things in order to feel the Breath of the Creator moving within—only then may the soul evolve. It is the Breath of Creator that brought us all to being: animals, sky, earth, water, trees, human beings, and so on. It is through this sacred breath that we are all related, hence why we use the term *All My Relations*. By respectfully uniting with this sacred Power within and around ourselves, we are able to transcend and work in harmony with All Our Relations.

Concept of Evil

In Native American tradition, there is no concept of sin. Instead, we believe that the vast majority of people are born good. The Good Red Road has a concept of evil that I will not detail here, but it simply points out to us as individuals and as a global community that which is grossly out of Balance and spurs us to restore harmony. We do not view ourselves as the ultimate creation but simply as another one of many creations. I've heard it said many times as I was learning the ways of the Red Road that we are no greater than the ants and no less than the mountains.

Reincarnation

We also believe in reincarnation. However, once again, humans are not at the top of the incarnation scale. We would not understand limiting the Great Spirit. The *Great Spirit*, who is also called the *Great Mystery*, is all-powerful and beyond our simple comprehension. Say, for example, that one needed to learn patience and how to listen but, lifetime after lifetime, stubbornly refused to master the lesson. Then there could be one incarnation in which the Great Spirit makes that individual come back as a tree. There that person would learn to "listen" with their entire being. They would learn how to extend equally into Earth Mother and stretch up Sky Father in Balance in order not to fall. The soul would benefit from learning many countless lessons that could only be experienced by being a tree. In the end, the teachings say that we are *not* humans having a spiritual experience but rather spirits having a human experience. Since the Great Spirit is limitless, we believe that our beautiful Earth Mother is not the only place with life. Indeed, she is considered to be a "college" within a much greater multidimensional "university."

Medicine

One term you may hear frequently in regard to Native American spirituality is the word *Medicine*. In its strict traditional sense, it is the spiritual or psychic ability that is bestowed on an individual by the Great Spirit. The strength of the Medicine depends on how much Power, or Breath of the Great Spirit, the person could channel while employing this ability. However, in my opinion, Medicine also includes the set of talents that each one of us uniquely owns. For who is to say which abilities are more important? The ability of talking to spirits and giving peace to the dead, or the ability to bring lightness of being and humor to a very tired world? For the sake of avoiding confusion, in this book I will stick to its traditional definition, which is that of spiritual or psychic abilities plus what I define below.

Medicine is still unique in its expression depending on the individual. Think of it this way: two people give you the same advice, but their worldview and who they are connected with on the spirit side affect the flavor and perspective from which this counsel is presented.

Another manifestation is its embodiment in an object blessed for a specific purpose or a sacred spirit who has a unique set of qualities. In the Native American tradition, they can overlap. Say, for example, a talking stick is being created for the purpose of helping to create community and promote teaching. Say that it is determined that the Wolf is the spirit that wishes to be honored to assist in this task. Some of the qualities of Wolf Medicine are those of the teacher and protecting its pack. The talking stick would be crafted with symbols of the Wolf. The item would then be ritually blessed, which includes asking the Wolf spirit to endow it with the qualities or Medicine mentioned above. The talking stick would then hold Wolf Medicine.

Heart

The concept of *Heart* is so fundamental that without it you cannot proceed upon the Good Red Road. In this tradition, you would not be able to function as a healthy and whole person without being in constant connection with your Heart. This is *the* place where the Great Spirit lives within you. It is where you connect with your sacred self, the Creator, and All Your Relations. Many people confuse Heart with emotions, and others say that it is intuition. They are wrong. Emotions and intuition are *expressions* of Heart, but they are not Heart. When you have been out on a beautiful day and feel in that moment completely at peace within yourself and connected to All That Is, we say that you have "touched the face of the Great Spirit."

Your Heart is where your soul dwells. It is never wrong. It has a Knowing that defies the chattering of the mind and goes beyond the waves of emotions. You can only find and hear it by going deep within yourself into what we call the *Great Silence.* Energetically, it resides where your physical heart is and includes the solar plexus. This is where the *throne of your soul* is located in your body. The teachings say that your Heart is like a chief who will guide you unerringly. Your mind is meant to be like the council to the chief. The mind is supposed to interpret what the Heart expresses and not try to dominate nor suppress it. I know that is very difficult to do in a society in which the mind is looked upon as supreme. The mind, however, can be fooled, and it can lie. Upon reflection of this topic, I came to the conclusion that the deepest things that move us and help us evolve are not logical, nor are they material, but felt and understood with the Heart. Engaging and reflecting with the Power of the throne of your soul, which is to say your Heart, is what allows you to journey between the worlds as a shaman.

The Seven Arrows

There are very Powerful divine beings that watch over us. They are known as the *Seven Arrows*, also called the *Seven Di-*

rections. The Seven Directions include the four *Great Keepers,* which watch the four points of the compass, and in the center are Earth Mother, Sky Father, and the greatest Arrow, the Great Spirit, who is within all things and beyond all things and who is found in the very center of the Medicine Wheel.

We always begin and end all prayers and rituals by thanking Them for watching over us and for guiding us in all our undertakings.

Medicine Wheel

The global concept of the sacred circle, which is the Sacred Hoop of Life, is found here also. The most common form of sacred circle amongst the First Peoples of the Americas is what is called in this culture the *Medicine Wheel.* A form of Medicine Wheel can be found in North America, the islands, and South America. It can be made of stones or simply drawn onto a ceremonial object. For many of the northern nations, it is commonly represented as a circle with at least two lines intersecting through the center. For islanders such as the Taino, it was simply a ring of twenty-eight stones with no lines going through the center.

The Medicine Wheel holds many spiritual teachings, and one of them is a foundational belief that to Walk the Red Road, one must be practical in both spiritual and physical aspects, which is why the ways of this path are very natural and simple. It is because of this belief that the Medicine Wheel acts both as an actual physical calendar of the natural world and also as a representation of the Great Spirit, people, and all beings of the natural and spiritual world.

Connecting with Nature and All Our Relations

Part of being a shaman is consciously walking in both the physical and spiritual worlds at all times with as much Balance as possible. One of the most important relationships you can develop is with nature. It is part of learning the practice that all things are connected. In all the traditions that I learned from, all of them emphasized being constantly aware of how the physical and spiritual realms interact and touch each other. Growing these relationships needs to be done on a daily basis and not just when you are journeying to the spirit realms.

A major step in reconnecting with Earth Mother and All Your Relations is spending time in nature. The steps of cultivating a relationship from a mere acquaintanceship to a deeper friendship and beyond are very similar here. Spending quality time daily in a place where a living element of nature can be found is critical for this sacred connection to develop. If you live in the city, parks or places where there are some potted plants and water fountains are where you can connect with nature. It is important also that you gaze upon the sky to make your connection with Sky Father.

Although it is preferable that at least some of these locations be outside in order for you to deepen your connection with nature, it can still happen inside of a building, but your progress will be slower. What matters is directly connecting with the elements of nature so that your spirit can become attuned to them and All Your Relations can be comfortable with you. I will go into how you can do this in greater detail further in this book. For now, take time whenever you can to relax and be still. Listen with all your senses and your Heart. It is not the length of time that matters as much as the quality and attention that you give to being fully present.

Walking in Balance

Another Powerful concept in Native American spirituality is the idea of *Walking in Balance*. What does this mean exactly? It has several meanings. It is learning to move through your life in such a way that you achieve inner harmony by creating a life that is the proper mix of healthy interactions in your public life and taking time for your private life. It is being in touch with yourself so that you achieve inner peace, while seeing how it relates to the greater picture. It is knowing when to act and when to be still. But for a shaman, it also includes the ability to Walk in between the physical world and spiritual realms. The shaman's job is to help create Balance wherever they may be. This includes helping an individual achieve Balance within themselves, within their community, and between the community and nature and with spirit beings. It includes bringing Balance to those in the spirit realm: for example, helping people cross over when they become earthbound.

Walking in Balance is a dynamic state much like walking with the physical body. Your body makes millions of microadjustments so that you can walk down the street—it is attentive to the demands of the terrain and your pace. Sensing this, your body will work harder at Balance as well as automatically adjust how much energy to use. It will signal the need for rest after much exertion. Your spirit body will do the same as you grow in your shamanic practice.

Part of learning to Walk in Balance means living mindfully. There are several ways to accomplish this. One way is being thoughtful of yourself and others so that there can be greater harmony wherever you are. An example of this is practicing common courtesy. It lessens the pollution of negative energy into the environment. Another simple way is to be fully present with whatever you are doing. I personally love a good cup of tea. When I am practicing mindfulness, I enjoy the cup of tea with all my senses. The rest of the world goes away, and I am grateful for having all my senses to enjoy that moment. I reflect on and envision the beauty and bounty of nature. I think about and send gratitude to the people who cultivated and harvested the plant. I thank everyone, including myself, who made it possible for me to be able to have that moment of rest while sipping something delicious.

Every day, take the time to be mindful of at least one thing that you participate in. Although seemingly trivial, it accomplishes three things: it helps you develop an attitude of respect and gratitude, it trains you to be able to completely focus on what you are engaged with at the time, and it makes you more attuned to all your senses as they become sharper, detecting subtle changes in your environment. These are important skills to have when you are developing your shamanic abilities.

Give as You Would Receive

I cannot stress enough how important it is in the Native American tradition to give as you would receive. If you wish to have help, and wisdom from All Your Relations seen and unseen, then treat them as you would wish to be treated. Learn about them and approach them with respect. As you would receive Medicine from them, be active in preserving and protecting Earth Mother. Our entire world is a sacred land, and the shaman understands that every step should be gentle so as to leave as little of an imprint as possible. You will find that if you do this when you do journey, your reputation of Walking in Balance will precede you, and those with whom you interact in the spirit realms will be much more receptive and welcoming of you. Your Relatives in nature will be there for you.

· THREE ·

Preparing Yourself to Journey

What precisely is *journeying*? It is when a person is able to send their consciousness and soul body into alternate forms of reality. This alternate reality is known as the *Dreamtime*. There are those who would say that meditation and journeying are the same thing. I disagree. Meditation is similar to journeying in that both can be guided. However, in meditation, the images and visions are controlled with the mind and can be altered upon command. Your consciousness and soul body remain intact here in this world. Sensations in your body can be easily correlated to suggestions given during the meditation. With journeying, on the other hand, you will find that you will have experiences and interact with beings that you had not expected nor can you explain. Messages and helpers that you meet while journeying in the Dreamtime will find a way of communicating with you here in this three-dimensional world. When you become proficient at journeying, you will feel that you actually are there physically in the spirit realms. Upon your return, you may find that what you've experienced in the spirit realms will remain with you, sometimes as physical sensations, in this one.

Just as with anything else, it's important to be in a good space when you begin to journey. Make sure you are rested, feel healthy, are well hydrated, are in a good emotional space, and have been eating nutritious food. You do not need to fast, but it is better if you do not eat heavily before you journey. Do not indulge in alcoholic beverages before you travel into the spirit realms, since they can interfere with journeying or, worse, leave you vulnerable to psychic and spiritual attacks. The use of illegal street drugs, misuse of prescription drugs, or abuse of sacred drugs are forbidden on the Good Red Road. Check that your energies are as Balanced as possible.

I would like to share a few exercises with you to help you become energetically Balanced. With all these exercises, please make sure to be in a comfortable space where you can be alone for a short period of time. Make sure that you are free from distractions, especially electronic ones. It should be a place where you can sit in peace and quiet.

In Native American tradition, we view Power as neutral. How we use it determines if it manifests as good or evil, order or chaos. Therefore, when I write *positive energy* or *negative energy,* I mean them in that sense. Read each exercise thoroughly before attempting it. You need to be familiar with every step, since you will have your eyes closed for most of it.

OVER-POSITIVE EXERCISE

The first exercise will be how to handle when you are feeling over-positive. You know you have an excess of positive energy when you feel as if you are constantly edgy and full of nervous energy, and you can't slow down. It is very much like when someone has too much sugar or caffeine. It is when you are restless and can't seem to relax no matter what you do. Or, as I like to say, when your bow is strung too tightly! Make sure to sit so that your legs are touching each other but not clenched. Your

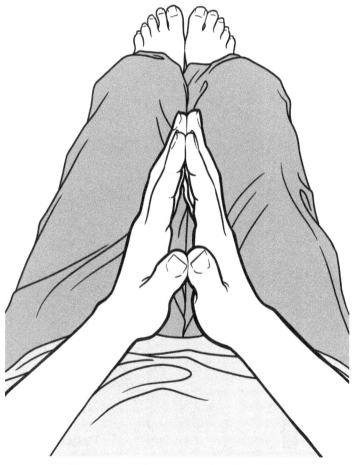

Figure 1: Over-Positive Exercise, Above View

Figure 2: Over-Positive Exercise, Side View

hands will be in what I call a relaxed prayer position. Put your hands together as if in a prayer posture in front of your chest and then let them relax. There should be a space between your palms, and your fingers should very naturally fan apart from one another. Your hands should naturally point at an upward angle.

Close your eyes. I want you free and able to bring to mind and Heart all those people and things that cause you stress, tension, and unrest. Breathe naturally. Feel the energy and emotions building up and send that down your arms and into the palms of your hands. Do not let your hands come apart! Exhale forcefully to the count of seven while envisioning that excess energy leaving through your fingertips into the sky. Hold your breath for a count of four. Breathe naturally until the energy builds up again. You will be doing this cycle a total of seven times. Every time you forcefully exhale to the count of seven, focus on releasing through your fingertips all those things that are creating this unrest within you.

What you are doing is releasing excess energy into the heavens. We say that Sky Father will purify the energy and send it to where it needs to go. In Native American tradition, the number seven represents the Seven Directions. Holding your breath for a count of four honors the Four Directions and is a number of stability. By doing this you are releasing excess energy and giving it back to the universe so that someone in need of energy may receive it after it is purified by Sky Father. You will know that you've done this properly because you will feel clearer and more relaxed. You will finally be able to breathe more easily!

OVER-NEGATIVE EXERCISE

Sometimes the opposite is true, and you feel over-negative. You know you feel over-negative when you just simply can't seem to wake up that day, feel foggy, and cannot seem to gain energy no matter what you do. Even though you are healthy, you still feel drained.

Sit comfortably but make sure that your legs are not touching. Rest your hands on your lap and have only your index finger and your thumb of each hand touching each other. The point of your index fingers should naturally go between your legs and slightly toward the ground. Close your eyes. Call to Heart and mind all those people and things that are draining your energy. Focus and direct that draining energy down your arms and into your hands to the tips of your index fingers. You will feel the need to take in more energy. Exhale naturally. When you inhale, do it forcefully for the count of five, completely filling your lungs; hold for the count of four, and then breathe normally. Repeat this cycle five times.

In the Native American tradition, it is taught that we are made of five elements: fire, which is energy; air, which is thought and process; water, which is Heart; earth, which is physical body and environment; and spirit, which is soul and transcendence. When you breathe in, you actually are recharging each of the elements. The number four, as stated earlier, creates stability. Releasing your negative energy to Earth Mother allows her to turn your emotional crap into purified energetic fertilizer. After this energy is cleansed, someone who perhaps needs to calm down will be gifted this energy you have recently released.

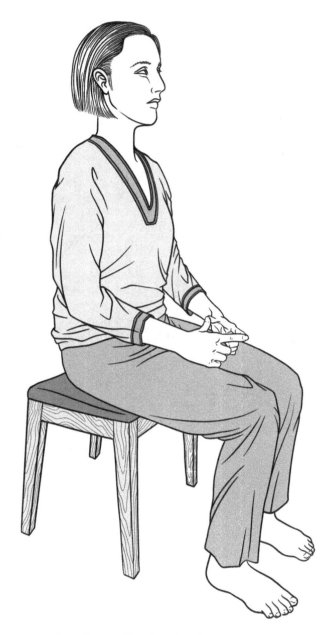

Figure 3: Over-Negative Exercise, Side View

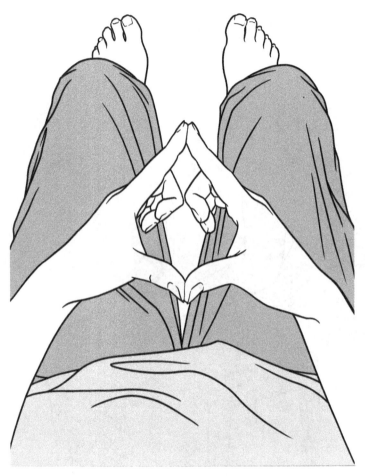

Figure 4: Over-Negative Exercise, Above View

Just as the physical body will only take in as many nutri-
ents as it needs, so your spiritual body will do the same with
these exercises. If you're not too sure if you are over-positive
or over-negative, then do both exercises. Nothing but good can

come from it. Indeed, if you do them both, you are honoring the sacred circle of giving and receiving equally, which is an important practice on the Good Red Road.

WATERFALL EXERCISE

The final exercise I will give you is a practice called the Waterfall. This practice allows you to connect evenly with both Earth Mother and Sky Father. It will allow you to truly connect with the Great Spirit within you and All Your Relations. Doing this will allow the sacred Power that is pure to flow through you. Performing the Waterfall will benefit you in shamanic practices and any other disciplines you follow. This is because you will not become exhausted since you are not using your own life force but instead harnessing pure universal energy for your tasks. Another benefit is that the Waterfall protects you from those beings that would like to latch on to your energy in order to attach themselves and drain you. This practice also shields those you're working with from (as I call it) your "psychic backwash"; this keeps it from touching others so that you do not accidentally harm them. This exercise has survived the ages and in turn will preserve you as you begin your Walk upon this traditional shamanic path.

Once again, sit in a quiet place with no distractions. As long as your feet are flat on the floor and you are comfortable, you may place your hands as you wish. Relax and breathe naturally. Feel your breath as you breathe in. Notice how your breath feels good as you inhale and it moves over your breastbone. Allow yourself to be completely lost within your breath. Focus on relaxing all the muscles in your face, in your body, in your arms and hands, down your legs, to your feet, to the tips of your toes. Breathe naturally and deeply. Focus now on the good earth beneath your feet. Feel her energy, the energy of our Earth Mother, rising through the soles of your feet and up your legs. This energy should feel good, warm, and very comforting. With every breath, draw that energy up to fill your body, filling your arms and hands to your fingertips. As you breathe in, focus your attention on your heart beating. Be within your heartbeat. Allow the sacred energy, this sacred "water," to fill every part of you until it goes through the crown of your head, where, on its own, it continues to flow upward and touches Sky Father.

This sacred energy will flow on its own from the sky back down into the earth. From the earth it will once again flow into the soles of your feet, filling your Heart, through the crown of your head. As you breathe and feel your heart beating, let your focus be completely taken by the sacred flow of Power as it moves from the earth, through you, into the sky, and back again. Relax and allow yourself to become part of this flow while it strengthens your Heart. Let your awareness feel the strength of your own spirit, the Light of Great Spirit within you, and your connection to All Your Relations.

You know you have done it properly when you feel relaxed yet alert, grounded, and energized at the same time. This flow of sacred "water," the Power of Creator, is very much like the flow of water as studied in natural science. Just as water goes from under the earth and finds its way to the surface and ultimately to the sky, which in turn will precipitate back down to the earth, so it is with this Waterfall. You will find that in the beginning the boundaries of your Waterfall will naturally fall a little bit outside your auric field. As you become adjusted to it, you will find that you will be able to make your Waterfall stronger and the area it encompasses around you will be larger in proportion to the flow of Power.

Make sure you go through this checklist of exercises before a journeying session every time. It will guarantee that you are in the best condition to succeed in your shamanic practice and gain greater health in body, mind, and spirit in your lifestyle.

· FOUR ·

How to Journey

One of the spiritual gifts that a shaman must be adept at is that of journeying. It is this ability that allows us to walk between this physical realm and that of the spirits. Through journeying, you will be able to directly connect and communicate with your sacred helpers and the healing energy that is offered to you. During this time, it is important to learn how to correctly interpret what you have experienced and any messages that have been given to you. When a person is proficient in the basic techniques of moving easily between the worlds with accuracy and discernment, then they are ready for further training. This further training includes methods that permit a shaman to be a living bridge to bring helpful spirits and benign energies from the worlds unseen into this one. Beyond this, one can also help both the living and the dead by guiding them to where they need to be on their path. In these advanced lessons, an individual learns how to access where there is imbalance and what practical steps need to be done to restore harmony. Your teacher and the type of healing they specialize in determine which tools and Medicines you master over time.

The method for journeying that I describe here is the same method that you will use regardless of which realm you will be traveling to. I will describe the different worlds of the Realm of Lower Earth, the Middle Realm, and the Sky Kingdom in detail and how to journey to each one in chapter 6. I ask, however, that you complete and become comfortable with how to journey first. Developing a strong foundation in your practice and making it second nature now will help you avoid frustration later. In Native American belief, everything is a sacred circle. So it is important to remember that it will be the same steps to return to this world as it was to go out into your journey, but in reverse sequence.

Gather What You Need to Journey

Make sure that you are in a good space in body, mind, and spirit. Don't forget your smudge and smudge feather. Prepare what you're going to use as a drumbeat or flute music to journey with and to call you back. It will be easier for you to journey if there is a drumbeat, although I do have some students who like to use Native American flute music. Especially in the beginning, it is okay to use a soundtrack that is devoted to shamanic journey. As you build your stamina, you will find that you will be able to journey for longer periods of time. It is very useful if the music or drumbeat has a point that signals when it is time for you to return. I have a free audio support that you can use on my website at eagleskyfire.com.

Set Your Intention Before Journeying

In everyday life, you set an intention of where you would like to be when you travel and what you would like to accomplish once you get there. It is equally important to focus on this and where you would like your end destination to be on the spirit side. When you first move into a new area, everything is unfamiliar and you have no idea where anything is, but the more you travel within it, the more familiar you become with the inhabitants and where to find what you need. The same will be true as you venture more into the spirit realms. When you complete chapter 6 and have journeyed at least once to each world, you will then have an idea how to select which one to travel to. For now, you are in the beginning of your practice exploration, and being able to consistently reach a realm is sufficient. The important thing is to get into the habit of setting a clear focus on what your goal is and which realm you would wish to reach every time you journey.

Purify Your Space by Smudging

A final preparation that is imperative is purifying your ceremonial space and yourself by *smudging* before traveling in between the worlds. Smudging is also called *blessing off*. This ritual serves the practical function of putting you psychologically, mentally, and emotionally in the right space. From a spiritual standpoint, this is a formal request to the Seven Arrows to create a sphere of protection and assistance while you are practicing your shamanic techniques upon the Good Red Road.

Smudge is also the name for the aromatic herbs that are bundled together. Everything in the smudging ritual has a meaning.

The herbs that are burned carry the raw essence of the prayers. The most common bundles are made up of cedar and sage. Cedar and sage are like a sacred couple because their energies complement each other. Sage takes away that which is not necessary. Cedar brings in that which is needed. Burning them together honors the Balance between the divine masculine and the divine feminine. The feather represents the manner in which you would wish for your prayer to manifest. A wild turkey feather is one of the easiest feathers to acquire. The turkey feather represents that you are coming in the spirit of innocence, fellowship, and goodwill. The fire that is used to light the herbs represents the Breath of the Creator. The smoke is sacred because it is the Breath of the Creator made visible.

The Seven Arrows and Their Gifts

Here I will describe each of the Seven Arrows and some of their most prominent traits. These traits are the lessons and spiritual gifts that they bring to us. What I share here only scratches the surface and is by no means exhaustive.

- The *Spirit Keeper of the South* helps us see the world without preconceived notions. This Arrow opens your eyes like the eyes of a child. This is the direction of creativity, discovery, innovation, and laughter. The Spirit Keeper of the South brings the gifts of innocence, fellowship, and goodwill.

- The next Arrow is the *Spirit Keeper of the West*. It is the place of going beyond fear and death. The power of transformation that comes from successfully moving through the storms of life. The west is the place of going into the Great

Silence to hear the Voice of the Creator within you. This Spirit Keeper watches over the place of dreams, which is the beginning of manifestation.

- The next Sacred Arrow is the *Spirit Keeper of the North*. This direction watches over the pathways that lead into the sacred realms. It is the place of ancient wisdom, of connecting with our Sacred Ancestors and divine beings.

- The *Spirit Keeper of the East* is the Arrow that watches over the Breath and Fire of the Great Spirit. It is the energy of a new day and new life. This is the direction of beginning a new path and seeing everything as if for the first time once more. This Spirit Keeper helps you see the details of a situation or relationship and how it might impact your future.

- *Earth Mother* represents the divine female face of the Great Spirit. Like a good mother, she not only gives us material things for us to survive but nourishes us with all that we need so that we may thrive in body, mind, and spirit. She brings stability and foundation.

- *Sky Father* represents the divine male face of the Creator. Like a good father, he teaches us when to speak and when to listen, when to act and when to be still. His face is ever-changing, reminding us that life, although dynamic, can still be peaceful and beautiful despite the winds of change.

- The last Sacred Arrow is the most important of all: the *Great Spirit* who dwells within you and in all things. The Great Mystery is in all things and beyond all things. All things come from and ultimately will return to the Creator.

SMUDGING EXERCISE

Meditate upon these teachings as you begin to offer the smudge. Which tribe's tradition you are following determines which compass point you start in. In the Taino Nation, they start all their ceremonies, including the smudging ritual, by facing the south since it is a place of innocence, like that of a child. This is the practice that I use for all my rituals. Since you too are in a "state of innocence," I ask that you begin there. The smoke is fanned by a feather as you move it around you. Light the smudge so that it gently smolders and offer it to the Seven Directions: the four compass points (make sure you close your circle!), Earth Mother (fan the smoke at your feet), Sky Father (over your head), and finally the Great Spirit (over your own Heart).

As you offer the smoke to the Seven Directions, it is important to understand to whom you are offering this smudge and why. It is not merely the reciting of words but connecting with each of the Spirit Keepers with an open and pure Heart. Fan the smoke four times in the direction of the Spirit Keeper that you are offering it to while at the same time focusing on the gifts and your request for protection. Be still for a moment and connect with the energy of that Arrow before turning to the next Sacred Direction. We always turn clockwise, turning toward the right, for that mimics the movement of Father Sun in the sky. This is the way of order and harmony with the natural world. Sit quietly and feel the energy of the Medicine Wheel that you have now created around you.

The ashes that are produced from burning smudge should never be thrown out! It is considered highly disrespectful. The ashes need to be given back to the earth. If you cannot bury them, then offer them with a prayer of gratitude and cast them into the wind. However, you may also place the ashes in the soil of a potted plant. (I have observed that this seems to act as an energetic plant food. Do not be surprised if that particular plant suddenly has a very healthy growth spurt.) As always, on the Native American path, giving the ashes back to Earth Mother has both a spiritual and practical component. From a spiritual standpoint, offering the ashes back to the earth is like honoring the life of a soldier who gave their life to protect you. The plant gave its life to carry your prayers. It is also a way of Balance. As the smoke has carried your prayers to heaven, the ashes act like seeds that ask for your prayers to become manifest here on earth. From a practical standpoint, giving the ashes back to the earth nourishes the next generation of plants. It closes the Sacred Hoop of giving and receiving equally.

If you cannot burn smudge, you can buy it in liquid form. You can usually purchase it at a holistic or metaphysical shop, at a health-food store, or online. Typically, the brands that offer liquid smudge honor the Sacred Hoop, which is to say they are eco-friendly and socially conscious. Spray the essence into the air in the direction that you are facing and fan the offering to the Seven Arrows with the feather as if it were smoke. Follow the same routine to offer the liquid smudge to the Seven Directions as described in this section.

JOURNEYING

It is time now to make sure that your energies are Balanced in case you need to do the over-positive or over-negative exercises before you proceed further. Focus on relaxing every single part of yourself. Relax your eyes and the corners of your mouth. Loosen all the muscles in your shoulders, your arms, and your hands, down to your fingertips. Focus on your breath as you breathe in. Notice how that sacred breath feels as it goes over your breastbone. Soften your belly and your back, relax every muscle down your legs, your feet, and your toes. Your feet will naturally connect more deeply with the ground beneath you.

Begin your Waterfall. Let your senses be completely taken up by your breath and with the sacred flow of Power moving through you, connecting you to Earth Mother, Sky Father, Great Spirit, and All That Is. Begin to focus that energy and feel it within your Heart. Feel and envision this Power as a bright light or fire within your Heart. Let your Waterfall fuel and strengthen this Sacred Fire within. Feel and envision this sacred light growing until it encompasses you. You will feel this Sacred Fire strengthening your Heart and cleansing your entire being. Call to mind and Heart where you are journeying and why. Walk through the Sacred Fire while calling your Guardian Spirit to you. Ask your Guardian Spirit to assist you in reaching the spirit realm you are traveling to. Once you reach that place, pay close attention to the energy of it. Note how it makes your body feel and how it touches your spirit. Be respectful of where you are and who you may encounter. When you're ready to return, express your gratitude in being allowed to be in this other place. Ask your Guardian to assist you once more to return to the fire of your own Heart. Feel your Heart beating and your own breath. As you exhale, release any excess energy and the Waterfall. Feel every part of your body and enjoy the feeling of relaxation and connection. Open your eyes and allow yourself to fully come back into yourself.

The reason we begin and end a journey by moving through the Sacred Fire in my tradition is to protect you and the spirit beings. As you move into the spirit realms, this Sacred Fire ensures that anything that belongs to this realm remains here. The Sacred Fire burns away and restrains any energy or being that tries to follow you without your consent. Consider this to be one of the original firewalls, just like the one you have on your computer. This is a critical safety measure, so *never* skip it!

Now that you know the basic steps of this dance, it is time to begin your first formal journey.

Your Guardian Spirit

It is time that you formally meet your Guardian Spirit, or Guardian for short. It is important that you understand the roles that your Guardian plays. Your Guardian Spirit was given permission from the Great Mystery to Walk with you before this incarnation and during this life and to *only* leave you upon safely escorting you back to the Creator.

Your Guardian Spirit has four basic jobs to assist you with your growth. The first one is as it sounds: protector. Your Guardian is to protect you even from yourself if necessary. The second job is a screener. You should only allow other beings or entities approach you after they are first cleared by your Guardian Spirit. This is an important safety practice that will keep you from harm or trouble as you go forward into the future. Another job is one of acting as an interpreter. If you think about it, even here in the physical world no other creation uses language like human beings do. The vast majority of living beings on this planet use other forms of communication that include scent markings, visual cues, and body language in addition to uttering different sounds. So, if you can imagine that on this planet we are the only creatures that speak the way we do, you will find this true exponentially as you venture forward into the other realms. When another being that does not speak nor communicate in a way that you can decipher approaches you, your Guardian Spirit will be able to interpret what they are trying to convey. Sometimes your Guardian Spirit will send you memories of your own life that will parallel a story or an energy similar to what the approaching being is trying to relay. This will help you avoid misinterpretations as you go forward into the future. The final duty your Guardian Spirit holds is one of acting like a bouncer. If there are energies and entities that become unwanted by being insistent and disrespectful of your time and space, regardless if they are harmful or not, the One Who Watches Over You has the task of removing them.

At times, feeling your Guardian Spirit can be very difficult. Why? That is because the One Who Watches Over You needs to be *perfectly* in sync with you. In the beginning, it is not uncommon for this benevolent being to use your own mental voice when communicating with you. This is because it is the one voice that, try as you might, you cannot help but hear. You can differentiate your own thoughts from the those of your Guardian Spirit because although your own internal voice is being used, the thought patterns and speech patterns will be different from your own.

Your Guardian will *never* be degrading, harmful, destructive, or threatening. It will *never* try to override nor take over your will. However, as you build a relationship with your Guardian Spirit, this being will be able to use its own voice and show you its true form. In the Native American tradition, not all Guardians are angels. Some may be Sacred Ancestors, and others may be sentient spirit beings from the different realms or sacred beings of nature. In addition to your personal benevolent ancestors, Sacred Ancestors of the Land, such as the spirit of a mountain or a river, can also choose to act as personal Guardian Spirits.

JOURNEY TO MEET YOUR GUARDIAN SPIRIT

Go through the procedures for preparing to journey as I have stated earlier. The first spiritual world that you will visit will be the Fire of Your Heart. When you feel that the Sacred Fire is filling every part of you, call your Guardian Spirit to you. Open your Heart and your mind to sense the One Who Watches Over You. Do not have any expectations. Allow yourself to completely be in this moment of connection with your Guardian Spirit. The energy should feel extremely familiar, safe, and nurturing. Ask your Guardian for a way of being able to identify it. Ask if it has a name that it would like to be addressed by. Pay close attention to whatever impressions you receive. Identifying the unique energy of your sacred protector is much more important than receiving a name or getting a visual image. Ask if there is any message or guidance that your Guardian would like to give you.

You will know you are done when you feel that you are lovingly dismissed by your Guardian or you feel that you are drawn to come back into your body. As always, before you return, express your gratitude.

Moving Beyond Obstacles When You Journey

It is very normal to encounter some difficulties when you first begin your shamanic practice. Here I will describe the most common ones and how to overcome them.

Your Restless Thoughts

This is when your mind is constantly busy and incessantly chatters. A beginner's mind may misbehave and get in the way of journeying. Since modern culture deifies the mind and teaches that it should be in charge at all times, you may find that your distracted mind will be resistant to being told to be quiet and listen to the Heart.

Set Expectations

If you found that you had difficulties when you first tried to journey, this is normal. I would like to share a bit about my own experiences when I was a young apprentice. It seemed as if all the other apprentices who were training were able to see their first journeys like a Hollywood movie with panoramic vision with full color and sound. Do you want to know what I saw? The inside of my eyelids! Yep, that was all. I was so disheartened. What I could do spontaneously as a child I seemed to fail miserably at when I attempted to train, no matter how hard I tried. I remember wanting to give up, but my Medicine Teachers at the time would not let me. The elders gave me encouragement, but the frustration in my Heart grew into reproachful self-anger. I will never forget the one moment that changed everything.

I was so consumed with self-pity and deep frustration that I had begun to shut down my abilities. One of the elders, a clan mother, approached me to give me a private one-on-one lesson.

I was so aggravated at the thought of yet another embarrassing failure that I was borderline disrespectful. I just wanted to be left alone! However, she would not leave me alone nor let me leave until I tried once more to journey. Fine. I just completely gave up and I decided that I would just go through the motions to humor her. Much to my surprise, that was the first time that I truly journeyed with focus and purpose. The training to harness my abilities had not failed after all!

With silent tears streaming down my cheeks, I stared with wonder at my Medicine Teacher. She smiled and gave me a hug of joy. She said the reason that I was finally able to do what the elders always knew I could was because I had thoroughly let go of *all expectations, including the ones I was imposing upon myself.* It was when I had totally surrendered that my mind had moved out of the way so that my Heart was given the space to be able to create a permanent breakthrough.

To this day, I thank them so much for not giving up on me as I would have done to myself! So if you find that you had some difficulties, persevere and do not lose heart. Perhaps you are a late bloomer like me.

Fears

Most of the obstacles come from within, and many of them are fear-based. A common one is the fear of being wrong. This is a fear that is usually instilled in childhood—fear of appearing foolish or that somehow you will not receive love and acceptance if you do not give the "appropriate" answer. The path of the traditional shaman is not separate from life but integrated throughout all aspects of it. And as we know about life, there is always more than one answer that can work to create a better

conclusion. The love of the Great Spirit and of All Your Relations is not conditional! As long as you come to this with realistic expectations, a compassionate Heart, and good effort, you
have nothing to fear.

This is followed closely by fear of feeling as if you are not
good enough. Usually, we are our own worst critics and are harsher
with ourselves that anyone else will ever be. Remember that this
is not just the practicing of simple exercises to build skills. It is
the developing of your own spiritual character and that of creating lasting alliances with benign beings in this and any other
world. The best gift that you can always give is to be who you
truly are, for only then can authentic relationships that are Balanced and healthy grow.

Loss of Control

A major fear that a great many people have is the loss of control. Sometimes trying to manage the fear of loss of control can
manifest itself as setting too many expectations when you come
to something that is currently unknown to you. The setting of
expectations, whether conscious or not, is an attempt by an individual to create points of reference with known parameters
that may have nothing to do with what is actually needed. It is
meant to be a safety mechanism, which is appropriate in many
circumstances but not in this one. I would ask you instead to
trade in your expectations, which will only get in your way, and
exchange them for learning to listen with your Heart, which
is working in partnership with a skeptical yet receptive mind.
There is also the advantage of working within a centuries-old
tradition. It offers the comfort of walking upon a well-known
path with built-in safeties to avoid and move beyond pitfalls. An-

cient traditions are practices that have been honed through the centuries to help you to grow securely through teachings that have been passed on for countless generations.

Too Critical and Judgmental

Other obstacles come from the imperious and endlessly noisy mind being too critical and judgmental and not wishing to relinquish control to the Heart. For many of you, it will seem odd to allow the sacred Voice Within, which comes from your Heart, to have more sway than your mind. Your mind may be tempted to dictate what this experience should look like and feel like. But here I need to dispel yet another myth, the myth that the logical mind and the Knowing deep within your soul should be kept apart. The truth is you need both halves to work together, both spirit and mind, in order to succeed on this path, just like you need both sides of your brain to work together to be a healthy person. However, the other extreme is also unhealthy. This is *not* about blind belief! It is important for you to remain receptive yet analyze and retain a healthy skepticism of what information is received, just like you do with any other area of your life.

Performance Pressure

Difficulty in journeying can also come from performance pressure. This is particularly true for people who are perfectionists and high achievers. Or you could be like me, feeling very self-conscious in the beginning of your training by comparing yourself to others who seemed to be able to move so effortlessly in between the worlds. In this culture, there is always pressure to succeed and to exceed expectations, which puts unnecessary stresses on you.

Be patient with yourself. Show kindness to yourself. Allow yourself to grow in your time, as the elders told me when I was first starting on this trail. Truly being able to completely relax in your own skin and trust your own Heart while getting accustomed to this sacred ritual takes time. It is also human nature that as the older we become, the more we expect ourselves to get it right the first time. Everything is a Sacred Hoop. There is a time for being the teacher, and then there is a time for being a student. The irony is the more you try to force "success," the longer it will take you to journey. I cannot emphasize enough to be kind and patient with yourself. *It takes time and much practice to discipline a mind that has never had to be subservient to your spirit.* Instead of stressing yourself out, enjoy this time of being a beginner, when the world is new once more with no preconceived notions. Allow yourself a sense of wonder as you begin to explore the realms as you have never seen them before.

Creating a Breakthrough by Daydreaming

I would like to share a technique that one of my dearest friends and students used to create her breakthrough. She found that if she focused as she was instructed but allowed herself to begin the process by daydreaming, her mind would be distracted enough to allow her Heart to take the lead. She would listen to the drumbeat and my guidance of the journey throughout the whole process so that she could transition from daydream to Walking between the worlds when her mind could finally let go.

This is because when you daydream, you allow your mind to drift off and be open while your body relaxes. This creates the perfect environment for your Heart to begin to take the lead. The key word here is *relax*! The difference between daydreaming and journeying is that you can completely control all aspects of a daydream, for it is a creation of your mind. Journeying, however, is a completely different matter, for it will take on a life and energy of its own beyond your control. Journeying is very much like living life. You make plans and focus on the manner of reaching your destination, but life itself will place different paths and events ahead of you that you may not expect. It gives you choices so that you have the opportunity to grow.

Journeying between the worlds is a personal experience. If you are a person who feels things better than you visualize them, you might find that your journey is one of sensations and impressions versus a panoramic scene. This is also true when you are developing your spiritual senses to connect with your physical ones. When we are first conceived, we do not have all our senses. The first sense we experience is touch, and then eventually the other senses develop one by one. So as you are beginning to Walk in your spirit body consciously, you might find that only one or two of your senses seem to be completely open. If you find that there are some senses missing, begin to focus on them. Gently allow for your conscious mind to catch up with the input given by your spirit body.

Remember, this is not you forcing yourself to create images of fancy and fantasy! This is training your conscious mind to be aligned with and receptive to your Heart. Your Heart acts as the conduit between your spirit body and your physical one. This practice impresses upon your consciousness whatever feelings or sounds you may have received on the spirit side and then disciplines your mind to allow the images to unfold on their own without you creating them. What also happens is that we expect for information to be communicated to us in the same way it is here on earth. At times you will find yourself connecting with beings or locations that are pure energy, emotions, or thoughts. In order to begin to overcome that feeling of being handicapped, permitting yourself to focus is the best solution.

Let me give you an example. Say that you get a brief sensation of a rocking motion. You also get the fleeting impression of cycles, but after that, there is only darkness and you have no idea exactly what you have experienced. All you know is that it is familiar somehow. You completely focus with your conscious mind on the sensations that you received on the spirit side. Slowly but surely, the image of an ocean develops along with the sound of the waves upon the shore. How do you know if it truly is a message versus monkey-mind chatter? If something is true, it will resonate within you like a bell. Even if you try to force a change in the energy, message, or image, it will either defy your efforts or revert back to its true form the minute you stop concentrating on it. The truth will always stand. It is okay to test what you receive. In fact, I encourage it. Your senses are more acute on the spirit side because they are able to perceive subtleties that can be easily missed by the five physical senses. It is best not to pressure yourself but let this ability unfold naturally with the help of lots of practice. It is not uncommon for people to not have all five senses for a while or perhaps not at all.

Be at peace and know that this is perfectly normal.

Other Reasons You May Not Be Able to Journey

Here are some common reasons why perhaps even after you have successfully journeyed, at times you might find that you are unable to. These are the most common causes, and they reflect whether or not you should continue to practice at that time.

Not Feeling Your Best

The first one is simply that you are not feeling well. Just like doing any other activity or exercise, you need to make sure that you are healthy, eating properly, and getting enough rest. Although it may not seem like it when you are doing shamanic work, you are using a lot of energy! As you journey longer and deeper, you will proportionately feel as if you have done the equivalent in physical exercise. As you grow in your practice, you will develop greater stamina in time. If you are overly tired or fighting off the beginning of some sort of illness, such as a cold, you will find it difficult if not impossible to go on the spirit side. Your body is a machine that is dedicated to surviving in the best possible way.

This is not to say that you cannot practice Native American shamanism if you have a chronic condition. The human body has a wisdom of its own. Your body will give only the energy it can safely spare in order to preserve itself. If you are fighting something off or if you are sick, then your body will redirect the energy toward healing and repairing itself versus a function that it does not feel is absolutely necessary for survival. The good news is that this is a great motivation for making sure that you are being consistent in your self-care. Just like athletes are careful to take perfect care of themselves so that they can be at peak performance for an event, so must you do the same when you are Walking between the worlds.

Unsafe Environment

Sometimes you are not able to travel between the realms because your energetic or spiritual environment might be unsafe or toxic. Your Guardian Spirit is in charge of making sure you have safe passage when you journey. In conditions like these, it is very much like air traffic control grounding the planes until there is safer weather for them to take off. If this is the case, then it is better to not force the issue but wait it out or go to a place where the energy is healthy and conducive to journeying. If you have correctly and consistently done the Middle Kingdom Exercise of Walking the Land, which I will guide you through in chapter 6, then you should have a sense that a place is not safe long before you have to be grounded by your Guardian. However, if you find yourself being held here on this earth plane, do not take it personally, for sometimes a place can seem beautiful on the surface but have something harmful hiding underneath it. Be confident in knowing that you are being well looked after!

No More to Find on the Spirit Side

Although this is not spoken of often, at times when you are not allowed to journey, it is because there is no more to be found or said on the spirit side in relation to what you are working on. At times like these, I like to say, "Do not look up into heaven, for your Guardians are sweating by your side here on earth." This means that there is no more to be learned or seen that can be relevant and useful on the spirit side. You have been given all the information you need, and the resources to begin to solve your problems or to move forward on a project are now here in this Middle Kingdom. Sometimes this can happen when we are

reluctant or are unsure of ourselves. It is normal to keep looking to one of the spirit realms for more and more information
until all that is left is the doing. On a positive note, when this
happens, take this to be an affirmation that you have everything
around you that you need in order to begin moving forward
successfully to completion. All that is left is the "doing" by ex-
ecuting a planned course of action after you are done thinking
things through!

· FIVE ·

Developing Good Relationships with Spirit Beings

Since there is a myriad of different entities, for the sake of simplicity I'll refer to them collectively as *spirit beings*. I think a good place to start our discussion on developing relationships with spirit beings is to help dispel some myths regarding spirit beings.

Spirits Are Not All-Knowing

The first myth is that all spirits are all-knowing. That is very untrue! The extent of a particular being's knowledge and perspective depends on where it hails from. For example, a Sky Teacher, considered an ascended master in this culture, would have a far greater knowledge of how your karmic lessons have impacted you throughout your lifetimes but would be very ineffective in telling you how to apply those lessons in a practical matter in the twenty-first century. Conversely, the spirit of your deceased grandmother may not understand karma, but she would be able to help you with the nuances of everyday life in a very personal way. Think of it in this way: just as you have go-to people in this life for help with technology, relationship advice, or just having fun, so it is in the spirit realms. As time goes on, you will build relationships with different types of spirit beings with a wide array of abilities and helpful knowledge.

Discerning Benign Relationships from Toxic Relationships

Another myth is that spirits help or hurt us merely because they can. This is untrue. We offer a friend or relative food, refreshments, and a place to be comfortable and sit when they come to visit. We do this so they can recharge and enjoy our company and hopefully want to visit again. The same is true of spirit beings. They may not ask for food or drink, but they need energy to be able to continue doing what they do. Different spirit beings require different types of energy. That energy will define and deeply impact you when you interact with them. There is good and bad everywhere. Here are some details to assist you in making good choices.

Regardless of where a relationship may start, whether it be in the Middle Kingdom or in any of the spirit realms, the same universal guidelines apply. A good relationship will be one of mutual respect and equal benefit. It will be one of open, honest partnership. Conversely, bad relationships are harmful and toxic. Typically, there is a dominance struggle for control, and it is destructive and self-serving. It is about abusive control and using any means to an end.

Here are some examples. Let's choose a benign sacred being, an angel, and that angel's mission is to promote peace on earth.

The angel will seek out individuals who want to live out that same purpose. In return for helping the angel with the mission of peace, that person's work will be enhanced. There will be other benefits. They may be blessed with extra protections and deeper insights that the average person will not receive. In turn, anyone who is assisting the angel will interact with others so that the energy of peace multiplies exponentially. This is how a single act of kindness can grow into a wave that creates global movements. The increase of joy, peace, and goodwill helps sustain the angel to do the work on earth, in addition to promoting its mission. Spirit beings that are good will always tell you up front what is expected of you in order to interact with them, whether it be for a one-time task or on a regular basis.

Much like good spirits "feed" on what is generated by helping to promote positive emotions and energy, evil and toxic spirits consume the opposite. They feast upon anger, pain, depression, and confusion, to name a few. Their relationships with people are parasitic. The idea is that a person is connected with others who in turn will be afflicted and multiply toxic energy and emotions. Once the host is no longer useful or is destroyed, then that evil being is able to follow the bonds of relationship and affect others the individual has been in contact with. Depending on the type of spiritual being, the spread of poisonous energy can become viral! Beings of evil and toxicity are just like a drug pusher who is trying to get you addicted—they will never tell you the price up front for their "assistance." Unfortunately, by the time a person figures it out, it is too late. Evil beings also like to masquerade as something benign in order to trick and seduce individuals into a trap. I will be covering different ways to help safeguard you as you venture forward into your shamanic practice.

How Spirits Are Drawn to Us

What attracts a spirit being to a person? For the vast majority of cases, like attracts like. A positive, happy, and peaceful person will attract spirits who also have the same type of outlook and energy. A negative, angry person given to drama will attract toxic and harmfully chaotic beings. Realize it is not just emotions but also your way of being from the inside that creates your auric field around you, which others will respond to whether conscious of it or not.

At times it can be that you have visited a place that has entities already "residing" there. Sometimes because of their curiosity or misguided way of trying to fulfill their desires, they will attach themselves to you, although they are not invited to do so. The beings range from a lost soul who doesn't know how to cross over to a curious nature spirit to an entity of ill will.

Although there can be other instances of how spirit beings attach themselves to someone, they are so rare as not to be worthy of mention here. Being aware of how you present yourself in this world or any other and being mindful of whom you invite to share your journey are usually enough to ensure that you make good choices.

Setting Boundaries

Another important element of creating healthy relationships is setting realistic boundaries. It is not very difficult. Set rules for spiritual beings that are similar to the guidelines you set for people in your life. Simple rules such as not interrupting you when you sleep or when you're in the bathroom might seem like common sense, but remember, you'll be dealing with entities who may not understand these concepts. Other good guidelines such as setting times you are available and receptive to receiving communications plus the spirit letting you know who is "speaking" to you are important. It will help reduce frustration on both sides!

Come with Respect

When approaching any spirit being, it is good for you to be mindful of your position. If you are approaching a deity or higher Being of Light, then remember that these are ancient beings that are much stronger and wiser than we are. Approaching them with humility and respect will go a long way toward having them respond to you when you request to contact them. Imagine how mindful you would be in approaching a head of state or a world spiritual leader. You are not worshiping them; you are merely giving the respect that is due for someone of that station who carries so much responsibility. For the spirits of the dead, or *Guardian Ancestors*, who are also known as *Hupia* in my tradition, approaching them with a good attitude and with honesty will go a long way toward them being receptive to you when you ask them for help.

SIX

The Realms and What You May Find There

The alternate reality of the realms, the space where we journey, is made of four "worlds." Several of my Medicine Teachers insisted upon developing precision in journeying. Just like you wouldn't think about driving a car without knowing how to operate it and safely navigate it from point A to point B, they insisted that the shaman know and understand how to safely journey between the realms. When you journey, you're going into the Dreamtime. In Native American culture, *Dreamtime* is known as alternate reality. Although each realm is composed of numerous levels, I will stick with speaking of the four major areas. I use the words *kingdoms*, *realms*, and *worlds* interchangeably.

Each realm vibrates at a unique frequency, and certain beings are native to each one. Becoming familiar with what to find in each world will make it easier to know where to journey to find certain types of information and to find appropriate energy as you need it.

The Lower Kingdom: The Realm of Deeper Earth

The first realm is the Lower World. It has nothing to do with a sinister netherworld nor infernal regions as it does in other cultures. Here is the place of deeply connecting with nature and finding your private personal sacred space on the spirit side. Some of the beings that reside here are Power Animals, Ancestors of the Land, and different types of elemental spirits.

The information and energy that are found here would be harnessed by a shaman in order to help a person Walk in Balance in both their physical and spiritual lives. It is a place to journey and to learn about one's own personal Power and how to responsibly use it. The Lower Kingdom is a place where you can go more deeply within yourself and understand how your current existence connects to your Dreamweave. The *Dreamweave* is the fabric of reality that is created through the will, karmic lessons, and the Power of the Great Spirit. It is also influenced by the results of our free-will choices as we interact with those lessons and the soul agreements we make not only with the Creator but with each other. The dreamcatchers that are so popular are one symbol of the Dreamweave. In the Lower Kingdom you can also gain insights to how a person's personal Dreamweave interacts, influences, and is influenced by the greater Dreamweave of the collective. Healing comes from the integration of the sacred seen and unseen within the self.

The Realm of Deeper Earth is a place where one can recover and become restored from the demands of everyday life.

JOURNEY TO YOUR SACRED SPACE

Just as you have places in the everyday world to relax and re-charge, so it should be that you have safe places on the spirit side. This is the place where you can always go in order to re-flect, receive counsel from your Guardian Spirit, or deeply con-nect with your Power Animal. It is a place for your own spirit to recover from the demands of life. Most commonly, it is a place found in nature. However, I've had several students over the years find a place on the spirit side that mirrors a place from this world that is located in a natural setting. The important thing is to *not* have a preconceived notion of what your sacred place might be. This will be your first journey to Deeper Earth, and not only is this where you will find your first sacred place, but it is the easiest for you to reach when first starting out. Focus within your Heart on how you want your sacred place to make you feel. It should make you feel Balanced and at peace. It is your private safe haven.

Go through the steps I mentioned in chapter 3 for prepar-ing for a journey. When you are within the Fire of Your Heart, ask your Guardian Spirit to take you to the Lower Kingdom. Feel and envision yourself going safely into the earth like water drifting underneath the surface. If you like, you can imagine touching and following the roots of a tree going underneath the earth. Breathe deeply and allow yourself to go further. When you arrive, pay attention to what type of landscape you have landed in. Here I use the term *landscape* loosely, for your landscape could be in the skies of the Lower World, deep be-neath the ocean, or in outer space looking at our Earth Mother. What matters is that you will know it because it will resonate deep within you. Since you are in a safe place, permit yourself to open every fiber of your being to connect with your sacred space. Let the energy of your sacred space on the spirit side flow and strengthen your life force on this side. Allow yourself to completely *be* in the moment.

As it becomes time to return, express your gratitude and begin to journey back to this Middle Realm. Record what you have experienced. It is a good practice to keep a journal to chronicle your travels on the spirit side.

I recommend visiting your sacred place at least once a week. Each time you return there, feel free to explore more and more of that territory. Remember that your Guardian Spirit is ever with you to help keep you safe. This is not meant to be simply a beginner's journey but a lifelong practice that will keep your spirit strong and healthy in the years to come.

In Native American spirituality, things must be both practical and spiritual. Just as you have begun to establish your sacred space on the spirit side and visit it routinely, make sure to make the same effort to visit a place in nature that gives you peace here in this Middle World. It can be as simple as walking through a park. The important part is to connect with nature in a mindful way. Walking as a shaman means consciously moving in the physical and spiritual worlds every day.

What Is a Power Animal?

A *Power Animal* is a spirit being, an animal of this natural world of earth or a mythical beast that is so filled with the sacred Breath of the Great Spirit that it has supernatural wisdom and abilities. I often get asked what my totem is. If I were to speak as a tradition keeper, technically, unless you are of Native American descent, you cannot have one. That is because a totem animal is a sacred creature who has divine connections with a specific tribe and bloodline. Claiming a totem would be very similar to someone walking up to a European person and saying that they would want that person's family crest and last name as their own because they find it pleasing. In the twenty-first century, the term *totem animal* is often used as a generic term meaning an individual's personal Power Animal, but they are different.

All people, regardless of heritage, have a personal Power Animal. The ancient teachings say that your personal Power Animal is the form that your soul would take if you did not have a human form. Any animal can appear to you from around the world. The myth that I would like to dispel is that somehow the animal itself has to be something big and powerful like a predator in order to have more Medicine. That is untrue! The spiritual leader and chief of the Taino has a black cricket for his personal Power Animal. It is not the physical raw strength of an animal that determines how much Breath of Creator it can carry. How far its essence or soul has evolved from a primal state determines how much Power, wisdom, sentience, and strength the Great Spirit will allow it to bear.

The more that you study your personal Power Animal, the more you learn about yourself. The more you interact with your personal Power Animal, the greater the connection with the sacred energy of that particular spirit being and your sacred self. Consider, for example, that the survival strategies of the wolf would be very different from the survival strategies of an ant or of a rabbit. All strategies are valid because they allowed that animal to adapt and thrive in its habitat. The reason for studying its natural behavior is that its survival strategies and what it needs to thrive very much mirror your own. Also study its environment in addition to its allies and enemies. Taking active steps in order to preserve the environment so that your personal Medicine can survive is a way of deepening your connection as well as showing honor and respect.

Mythical beasts upon very rare occasion can be the personal Power Animal of an individual as well. In these cases, study more about the lore and history of this mythical animal in order to understand its significance. Take for example the dragon. Dragons are found in every form throughout the world. The disposition of an Asian dragon is a highly intelligent, divine, and benign primal force connected to the movement of wind and water that brings good fortune to the righteous. In contrast, the dragon of Europe is one that could be good or evil. Like in Asia, they are very powerful Medicine, though in Europe they would call it *magic*. If they are good, then they are protectors and in certain European cultures can bestow magic upon those they favor. If this beast is evil, then it is an aggressive bloodthirsty monster with the desire only to conquer and to hoard treasure.

When I was younger, I adored tigers. They are graceful, powerful, exotic, and a symbol of leadership. In Indian and Asian traditions, they are revered and respected because they are seen as evolved beings. I desired those qualities so much that I wanted Tiger more than anything else to the point that I had thoughts of no other animal. At that time, I was studying with the Iroquois and the Seneca Nations. For these nations, the Wolf spirit is a very prevalent, Powerful teacher and totem to one of their clans.

When I journeyed, instead of ending up in the jungles, I ended up in the forests that were around me. What came to me was a Wolf. In my youthful ignorance, I was disappointed because I thought wolves to be so common. At that stage of my life, I wanted so much to stand out. I had the audacity to deny my first Medicine! Thank heaven that the Seven Arrows, the Sacred Ancestors, and my Medicine Teachers were so patient. My teachers at the time smiled and reminded me that the Medicine chooses you, you do not choose the Medicine, and in the end, I would surrender to it.

I was very stubborn and resisted it for a long time. The Wolf spirit found many ways to demonstrate that it was to be my teacher and my Medicine. One time we were almost run off the road by an eighteen-wheeler. The company that it belonged to? A company with *wolf* in its name. Another time I was going to buy food in town, and I almost tripped over a young boy at the entrance of the market who was selling popcorn. As I looked down to apologize, I saw that he was wearing a Cub Scout uniform with the wolf cub's head prominently showing on his kerchief. On yet another day I turned on the television and there was a nature program about wolves.

And so it went that I was hounded in this world and on the spirit side until I surrendered . . . just as the elders predicted. How glad I am that in the end the Wolf spirit did not give up on me and instead became one of my greatest teachers. With the guidance of the Wolf and my Medicine Teachers, I was taught the traditional ways and grew on the path of becoming a shaman, tradition keeper, and seer.

I share this story to reinforce that you should not have preconceived notions about which animal may choose you. You must surrender whatever prejudices you have, even if some of them come from a culture. For example, in the Western world, the snake is looked upon as a symbol of evil and deception. I think this odd, as in Western culture the symbol of medicine, the caduceus, is a staff with two snakes entwined around it. In most Native American traditions, no Medicine is all good or all bad. How and what you manifest with a Medicine reflects what is in your Heart and determines if it will be good Medicine or bad Medicine. The old teachings say that the Great Spirit intentionally created all the Medicines to have strengths and weaknesses. The Creator did this so that we have to be interdependent as a global family. We need each other, so do not look at disadvantages as handicaps! What one does not have, you do. What you do not have, another does. And so it is that we enter into a community both in this physical world and in the realm of spirit. There is a healthy strength in Balanced diversity.

So how do you find out who is your personal Power Animal? Perhaps you already know. It could be that you are irresistibly drawn to a specific animal species. Perhaps you notice that a particular type of animal has been drawn to you. Understandably, you may find it hard to distinguish if you are drawn to the animal merely because of your love for it or if the animal is actually your personal Power Animal. To remove all doubt, I will guide you on a journey to find out.

Journey to Find Your Power Animal

Now you are ready for your second journey into Deeper Earth. Prepare yourself for journeying as I have described previously:

make sure that your space has been blessed off as explained in "Purify Your Space by Smudging" in chapter 4, that you are well connected with your Waterfall by performing the exercise found in chapter 3, and that you are in a good space mentally and emotionally. Connect with the Sacred Fire of Your Heart as you have done previously in the section on journeying found in chapter 4. Set the intention of this journey by focusing with your Heart and your mind that the goal of this journey is to discover your personal Power Animal. Ask your Guardian to escort you and journey to your sacred space within the Lower Kingdom. Once you are there with all your being, call out to your personal Power Animal. Remember, do not have *any* expectations!

This animal may or may not choose to approach you the first time. Please do not be discouraged if you cannot see it clearly initially. When it does appear, it will show itself to you several times. In my tradition, we say your personal Power Animal will appear four different times to honor the Four Directions in order to demonstrate that it is coming to you in a sacred way. Ask permission of your Power Animal to approach it. At this point, I would like to say something to dispel another myth that I have run into, which states that any insect you see is an evil spirit. That is foolish! The most abundant animals on this planet are insects. We would be lost without them. So, do not reject insects even if you do not like them. Welcome a spider or a bumblebee warmly if one appears as your personal Power Animal. Connect and touch your Power Animal, note its gender if possible, and let it take you where it resides.

The place where your personal Power Animal resides will be your second sacred space within the spirit realms. Truly become one with it. If it is a bird, try flying with it in the boundless sky; if a fish, swim with it in the clear running waters; if a deer, bound with it through the pristine forest. You might even spontaneously shape-shift into that animal. If you do, congratulations! This is a sign that you are attuned to your personal Power in perfect harmony. When it is time to return, allow your Medicine Animal to connect to your Heart and be within the Fire of your being. You will know that it is time to return because you will feel like you are being dismissed from the Lower Kingdom or your Guardian will tell you that it is time to go. Make it a habit to return through the Sacred Fire of Your Heart before opening your eyes and becoming completely present in this world. Return with your animal into this world. In a way, you are not truly retrieving anything that has not been with you since your beginning. You are merely strengthening the bond with your personal Power Animal. As you learn the shamanic ways, this is your second safe, open, and stable connection between this world and the realm of the spirits.

Interpreting Your Power Animal's Meaning

Here I will briefly interpret what each of these types of animal means:

Bird: If you found that a bird came back with you, then you are connected more with the Sky Realm. You have a natural gift for seeing things from a bigger picture, which helps you solve problems in a practical way while preserving the essence of a project or relationship.

Aquatic: If an aquatic animal, including crustaceans, returned with you, then you are connected strongly with the element of water. You have an empathic ability and can sense what lies within the Hearts of people. You can "hear" what words cannot express.

Reptile: If a reptile followed you, then you will have easier access to ancient memory and understand the movement of primal forces within a person or situation. You will have a gift for creating ritual and preserving traditions.

Insect: If an insect chose you, this means that you have the ability to see things without the complications of emotions and are more readily able to see the process of how things can work. You will have the gift of sensing and interpreting global energy and connect to the collective consciousness.

Mammal: If a mammal went into your Heart, then how to live fully in this Middle Kingdom will be one of your strengths. Mammals focus on a specific character trait and how best to identify growing into your life purpose. You have the gift of being grounded and are able to communicate more easily with the beings that live in the Middle Kingdom.

Mythical: If a mythical beast responded to your call, this means you will have an easier ability to channel spiritual gifts but may have a difficult time grounding in this Middle Kingdom. You have an instinct for knowing what inspires people and carry catalytic force for change within you. You can't help but stand out in a crowd.

Crossover: The final classification of animals that I would like to cover is what I call *crossover animals*. These are animals that belong to more than one type. They have the advantages and disadvantages of both classes. Take the bat, for example. This is a mammal that flies through the air. The bat is a mammal that symbolizes being able to "see" and navigate through the darkest times of our lives. It does not use its eyes but sonar. It is very much like when we are going through difficult times and our normal ways of navigating or "seeing" our way through do not work. We must use other means to get through the hardship. Since the bat also has wings, it has an element of being able to connect more with the higher spiritual realms. In this case, the bat also gives us the gift to fly and navigate perfectly through unknown territory during the darker times in our lives. The bat is one of the helpers and perfect guides during times that are painful and require courage to go beyond where we have been. Ultimately, this animal will guide you from the darkness into the light by leading you to insights to explain why you are going through this experience and what lessons it holds. Although the bat may look scary, it will protect you in your hour of greatest need. It encourages us to use senses beyond the normal or go beyond comfortable thought patterns. It allows us to maneuver with as much grace as possible through unknown territories, especially through the dark night of the soul. The bat is the teacher of positive transformation through properly moving through adversity or the ending of an old life.

One thing I would like to mention is that a personal Power Animal will *never* be another human being, an elemental, nor a higher sentient being like a deity or Sky Teacher! Your personal Power Animal is representative of your essence in its most basic form. Working with your sacred animal strengthens you overall and your ability to ground on this earth while you are developing your spiritual gifts. It creates equal strength and Balance as you walk simultaneously in both the physical and spiritual worlds.

When Medicine Changes

It is upon rare occasion that a person's Medicine changes, and it is never a casual thing! It is *never* because an individual desires it. An individual's personal Medicine is more than just an identifier. It is the true essence of who they are, who they are becoming, and how they will move in the world. When a person undergoes changes so profound that their old Medicine no longer aligns with their soul, then the Creator assigns them a new one. It usually takes place over a long period of time when a person has undergone a series of deep transformational life events, powerful spiritual experiences, and mystical epiphanies. In addition to a person's spiritual energy changing, signs from this world and the world of spirits repeatedly indicate that a transformation is taking place. Wisdom elders and spiritual teachers are consulted. If they agree that a change is indeed taking place, then they guide the individual through various sacred practices to ascertain what the new Medicine is. Once the new Medicine is determined, there is further prayer and teachings given by the wisdom elders and spiritual teachers to assist that person in learning to Walk with that new Medicine and to understand the impact that it will have on their life and destiny.

After many years of being a spiritual teacher and ceremonial leader, I began to receive profound spiritual insights and teachings from the sacred spirits beyond what I had been given by my Medicine Teachers and elders.

I shared these different dreams, thoughts, and greater visions with my teachers and elders. I could feel a deep change was going on within me but had only equated it to the stage of life that I was in. I simply thought that this was the result of becoming more mature and following my desire to lead a more spiritual life by going further with my practices. All this was taking place in addition to having a busy schedule and devoting myself to be a good mom to my children. My teachers had seen a pattern that I had not. I was told that I needed go on Vision Quest. Vision Quest is a sacred rite of transformation and rebirth, and under the guidance of a spiritual teacher, you are prepared spiritually, emotionally, physically, and mentally to be able to endure this sacred retreat. Once your teacher says that you are ready, then you go out into the wilderness to a sacred place and fast for four nights and four days. While you are there you continuously pray and "cry" to the Great Spirit to grant you a divine vision.

Throughout my entire Vision Quest, only the Eagle consistently reappeared to me both physically and in the realm of the spirits. Connecting with the Eagle resonated deep within my soul and felt like a part of me. I experienced a deep communion with the Sacred Fire of the Great Spirit, as symbolized by the sun. At one point when I journeyed, I saw the Eagle sacrifice herself by flying straight into the sun, and she was burned away. She rose again as a Fire Eagle and she hovered in front of Earth Mother.

After returning from my sacred space, I shared what I had received on my Vision Quest with my spiritual teacher. He went to consult with other spiritual elders and teachers in order to determine the lessons I needed to learn that would guide me in growing with the Eagle. After a long while, when I demonstrated that I understood what I had been given and could Walk with this Medicine responsibly and in Balance, a simple ceremony was performed in front of the community to acknowledge and confirm the change in my spirit. At the time my elders and spirit teachers chose the name *Eagle Skyfire* for me. The Wolf is still with me and will always be a part of me as my teacher, helper, and guide.

Counterbalance Power Animal

I would also like to introduce a teaching that I have not seen written anywhere else. You have not only your personal Power Animal but also its complement. The personal Power Animal would be like your dominant hand, and it represents the most pronounced, familiar, and recognizable aspects of yourself. The Counterbalance Power Animal is not only the complement to your personal Power Animal, but it also represents the challenging side of yourself that you need to master to be a complete person.

I will use myself as an example. As I mentioned earlier, my Medicine is that of the Eagle spirit. The Eagle is known as one who oversees, teaches, and see things from a very high vantage point. They are interpreters of law and divine law. Eagle people are known to be very responsible, quite formal, and serious. They aspire to create higher standards for this world and want to help elevate it. People with this Medicine have to make sure that they do not become biased and believe that their standards are the only ones by which things should be measured.

My Counterbalance Power Animal is the Macaw. The Macaw could not be more opposite than the formal and dutiful Eagle! Indeed, there is a reason why the macaw is a symbol for Margaritaville! This noisy and playful bird believes that life should be a pursuit of relaxation and enjoyment. The Macaw is a sacred clown. While the Eagle tries to be very diplomatic, precise, and cordial while speaking, the Macaw is the opposite, using very casual, blunt street talk. Macaw Medicine just tells it like it is with few if any filters, and people with it sometimes get in trouble because they can be too direct.

Your Counterbalance Power Animal is the other half of yourself that you may not be as comfortable expressing, much like feeling awkward when using your nondominant hand. Know that mastering the Medicine and developing the gifts of your Counterbalance Power Animal will make you a more complete and well-rounded person. I would like to mention that the counterbalance does not have to be from the same kingdom or the same type of animal as your dominant personal Power Animal. Just because I have two birds does not mean that you cannot have a different combination.

Journey to Find Your Counterbalance Power Animal

Here would be your third journey into the Lower Kingdom. When you are ready, go again to a quiet place and make sure that everything was blessed off. Within the Fire of Your Heart, call your personal Power Animal to you. Allow your personal Power Animal to take and lead you into the Lower Kingdom where your Counterbalance Power Animal dwells. Observe where your Counterbalance Power Animal lives. Once again, respectfully ask permission to be allowed to touch and to approach it. You will recognize this sacred animal because just as before, it will show itself in at least four different aspects and will resonate deep within your spirit. It is quite normal for your Counterbalance Power Animal to be an animal that you might enjoy but that feels extremely awkward and hard to identify with. Remember, these are the other parts of yourself that need to develop in order for you to become a whole person.

I know that my Fire Eagle Medicine has finally learned to lovingly tolerate the Macaw after several years. The Macaw has finally stopped ribbing the Eagle . . . at least not as frequently. I found over the years that developing an intimate connection with both my sacred animals has helped me become strong in many ways. One of them is that I have become a formal speaker but have that earthy humor that everyone can identify with. Spend quality time with both your sacred animals. You will be well rewarded by being able to love all aspects of yourself equally.

From here on when I say to "ask your Power Animals to come with you," I mean both your personal Power Animal and your Counterbalance Power Animal. Depending on what's needed, one or both may show up for you to safely journey. If I ask you to "call your Guardians," I mean the collective that is made up of your Guardian Spirit, Power Animal, and Counterbalance Power Animal.

The Middle Kingdom: Our Home Realm

The second realm that I like to speak of is the Middle World. It is where we are right now. In addition to life as we know it here, some of the beings you would find here are earth spirits, souls in transition, and spirits who are earthbound. Here a shaman would be able to see a person's life lessons from a first-person perspective. Seeing a life from ground level, as it were, gives a more "human" perspective to why things happened as they did. Information and energy that comes from the Middle World can assist a person in feeling more connected with being here in everyday life. Since we reside in the Middle World, this is the easiest realm for a beginner shaman to journey through.

Being a shaman means consciously walking within the spiritual world and the physical world at all times. If you are to become a shaman or shamanic practitioner, it is imperative to strengthen your ability to be a bridge between the worlds. This begins by strengthening your connection with the land. Sadly, in modern society, the earth is just seen as an object. In contrast, the sacred connection between Native American people with Earth Mother is legend. For us, Earth Mother is a beautiful, divine feminine being and we are all her children. You may have noticed as you walk in different places that some feel friendly, others dark, and others welcoming, and still others seem to call you. Before we became so preoccupied with modern distractions, all our ancestors, regardless of where they came from, needed to pay close attention to what was going on in the natural world around them. Failure to do so could result in countless hardships and even the death of the whole tribe or village. We still need to be connected to the land and to nature. When we are disconnected from our natural environment, we feel stressed and alienated. You do not have to be living on the edge of the great wilderness in order to be connected with nature. For those who live in cities, walking through a park, sitting by plants in a shopping center or bus station, or even tending to the houseplant in your home along with a fish tank could do in a pinch. However, whenever possible, it is better to go outside to a park or other places of natural beauty.

Being an active bridge between the worlds is what gives a shaman the ability to bring messages and energies and act as an intermediary with the unseen and the divine. Just as a bridge has two abutments, you have to be equally strong in connecting with the energy of this physical world and of the spirits. Since we are residents of the Middle Kingdom, let's create the first abutment here. Just as we are body and spirit, so too is our native realm.

MIDDLE KINGDOM EXERCISE: WALKING THE LAND

Let us begin with something simple. This exercise should take between fifteen minutes and half an hour. Make time to visit a place of beauty in nature that is nearby. It is even better if you feel a special attraction to the place. It should be a location that you truly love, enjoy, and feel safe in. It is preferable that you go on your own since being with another person will distract you from this exercise. Go on a day when the weather is pleasant and you are not in a rush to go anywhere. Begin walking at a leisurely pace and pay attention to your senses one at a time. Listen to the ambient sounds on land and in the air. As you walk, feel the ground beneath your feet and the kiss of the breeze and sun upon your body and face. Pay attention to every detail of the landscape that is around you. Note the color of the sky and the shape of the clouds. What people or animals are around you? Breathe deeply and see if you can decipher the different smells that are surrounding you. Is there a certain taste that is in your mouth right now? Do not rush through this; with every footstep, you are sharpening your senses one at a time. Let your mind be open to receive the information that your senses are giving you.

Find a place to comfortably sit and allow your Heart to be open. Focus now on what is unseen. Once you feel that you can completely place yourself in this natural environment, begin to open your Heart and feel how this place touches you. What does the energy that is around you feel like? How intense is it? How much of it is of the land versus the people and animals that are upon it? What similarities and what differences are there between them? Breathe deeply and focus as these details come into your consciousness. Allow yourself to become immersed in this moment and sense your place upon the land. While you are thoroughly immersed in the vision and senses of this place of nature, allow yourself to connect even further with the land by sending love and gratitude. If you feel a warm and welcoming energy responding back to you and connecting through all your senses, this is the land responding to your call and strengthening its relationship with you. You may even feel emotions of joy and peace come rushing back to you. This is a very good sign! You have successfully begun a sacred relationship with this natural space. Give thanks for this moment and return to your regular activities.

Beginning your Walks with all your senses open and fully aware no matter where you are is a good habit to have. Only open your Heart in those places that you know are safe. This prevents unwelcome beings and energies from deeply touching you and attaching themselves to you. Remember that your goal is to move as a quiet observer. The more you do this in everyday life—whether it be walking through a park, downtown in a city, or in a quiet forest—the more you will be able to distinguish between the different energy levels of a place and how you might affect the people and animals that reside there, whether they are conscious of it or not.

This is an important skill to develop when you are walking as a shaman. This practice will teach you to pay attention to your environment and what might be moving within it both physically and unseen. This gets you in the habit of connecting and being completely aware with all your senses and your spiritual senses as you journey between the worlds.

Now you will build the second abutment of your bridge. It is time for another journey into the Middle Kingdom. Just as you carefully opened your senses and explored a favorite place in nature in this physical world, you will now explore the same location from spirit side. Go to your regular space for this journey. Make sure that you have blessed off the room and yourself. Ask for your Guardian and your Power Animals to be with you. Make sure that your Waterfall is strong and begin to focus on the Fire Within Your Heart. Ask your personal Power Animals to lead you to the place you physically visited within this Middle Kingdom. You may already feel that the land is calling you back to it. As you did in the previous exercise, use all your senses to connect with the land but focus especially on your spiritual senses to be open. Although you might know how the land looks and feels in the physical side, release yourself from all expectations. The landscape can look similar but have differences in its spiritual manifestation.

Pay attention to the beings of nature and the energy you feel there. You might find that they're more than just animals and trees. You might find that there is more than what you would expect in physical reality. The Spirits of the Earth may choose to show themselves to you. Some of them are the little people known as the *Jogahoh* by the Iroquois Nations. They have various names throughout many cultures, such as the *domovoi* in Russia, the *ebu gogo* in Indonesia, the *Patupaiarehe* of New Zealand, and the *fae* of Europe, to name a few. You might also see the Ancestors of the Land, the Grandmothers and Grandfathers who live within the trees and stones. If you should meet them once again remember that you are in their home. Express your gratitude for being allowed to be there and for being permitted to see them. Ask if they have any messages or insights for you. The important thing I am trying to teach here is to listen with *all* your senses both physical and spiritual at the same time!

Give yourself permission go deeper and connect further with the energy of that sacred space just as you did when visiting this place physically in the Middle Kingdom. Let only the spiritual energy of the land touch your Heart. Permit the energy of the land to dwell within your Heart so that it may come back with you. When your Guardians say that it is time to come home or if you are dismissed by the Spirits of the Land, give thanks and begin to return here. Open your eyes.

It would be good for you if you have a journal to record what you have experienced. As soon as possible after you are done with this exercise, physically visit the place that you journeyed to. Begin to walk with your senses open and correlate what you experienced on the spirit side with what you experience spiritually and energetically while walking upon the land. You will feel a very profound difference from the first time you visited this place.

In core Native American spiritual practice, this awareness and sacred connection are what allow us to Walk with respect and Walk gently upon the land no matter where we might be. For you who are beginning this sacred relationship, this identifies you as someone who is not ignorant and blind but someone who Walks with humility and who truly is beginning to learn how to See and Hear. You will find that the beings of nature seen and unseen will be very willing to talk to you in both the physical realm and in the spiritual realm. The more you practice this, the stronger the bridge you become by journeying between them. The strongest bridges take years to build.

Journey into Your Past Life

Let us begin your next journey into the Middle Kingdom. It is time to journey to the past life that has had the most impact on this current incarnation. I would like to mention, however, some sacred teachings and taboos in relation to past lives. Looking at past lives strictly for entertainment is forbidden. For although you would be looking at part of your own soul, it is still considered to be disrespectful to the dead. Whenever you journey to past lives, it must always be done respectfully and with a clear purpose. One does not disturb the dead lightly.

Each past life is like its own separate book in the greater collection of your soul's journey. They hold the lessons and experiences of the particular karmic lesson that Great Spirit is having you learn. You are to observe and not to relive the sorrows or joys of the past. I would also like to mention that initially, you might only get impressions. That is okay. As you connect to a past life and begin to link those memories with your current self, you will find that memories begin to pop up as time goes along. Different reflections, preferences, and prejudices of your past life will gently start coming into your consciousness, so be patient with yourself and let time unfold naturally as the memories come back to you.

Go to a quiet space and make sure to bless off yourself and your space. Make yourself comfortable and call your Guardians. Focus and strengthen your Waterfall. Relax and allow yourself to completely connect with Great Spirit within you, Earth Mother, Sky Father, and All Your Relations. Allow the sacred flow of life and Power to flow from your feet through your legs, filling your body, to the crown of your head and back again. Strengthen this divine flow so that you can really feel and envision this sacred light, the divine fire within your own Heart and soul. Strengthen that fire and let it fill every part of you. Call your Guardians to be with you in this sacred space. Focus your Heart and your mind, and focus on the purpose of the past life that you wish to visit. Ask your Guardians to take you to a place in this Middle Kingdom, back to the time you existed in relation you what are seeking to know. Open your Heart. See what impressions you have and if possible, see who and what is in your environment. Focus yourself in order to become oriented. Here are some questions to ask yourself:

- Are you human?
- What is your gender?
- How old are you?
- What are you doing?
- What time period and part of the world are you in?

Ask your Guardians to take you to a significant moment in that lifetime. Pay attention to how you were feeling, who was around you, and the elements that led up to that event. If you find that you are having difficulty sensing what is going on, then connect more deeply with your Power Animals. Since your Power Animals live in the realm of spirit, connecting with them will enhance your own spiritual senses and perceptions on the other side. After that, ask to be shown what significant lessons or talents in your current incarnation are from this past life.

Sometimes, if a memory is too painful, your soul will block it out. Do not push it! It is more important that you understand the lesson and the action surrounding that lesson than that you see the actual event. When you have seen and felt all that you are permitted to, your Guardian spirit will begin to call you back. Give thanks for what you were allowed to see. Come back with your Guardian Spirit and your Power Animals. Return into the Fire of Your Heart and this present time. Feel your body; breathe deeply and naturally. Allow your Waterfall to Balance and ground you back into your body. Be open to your Guardian and your personal Power Animals so that they may strengthen you and bring you back completely into this current time and space.

Study what you can from your past life. What era was it? What was your station in that life? Did your gender have an impact on what roles you were allowed to play? How much power did you have over your destiny in relation the culture? What fears, likes, and talents from that lifetime are different from those in this one? You will know that you have hit upon things correctly when they resonate deep within you. It will ring like a bell and feel like the truth. Do not make judgments on yourself from the past life. Understand it is a point of reference and meant to be a source of encouragement of where to grow. It can indicate which talents in this incarnation give you the most benefit to develop.

Use this technique if you wish to understand different aspects of how you behave or certain reactions that you have in this lifetime, especially if it does not correlate logically or psychologically to anything that you have done so far. I know that there are others who say that one can do releasing work in order to absolve oneself from past karmic debts. On the Good Red Road, we do not believe this. Life lessons and unfinished lessons are nothing to run away from. They are opportunities for your soul to grow and for you to develop your character. Embrace these lessons in a loving way by integrating what is useful. You will become spiritually healthier, and the wisdom ultimately will allow you to release the karma in a beneficial way since you will have mastered the lessons.

Sometimes people say that after they journey to a past life, they have a sensation connected to a certain part of their body or even to a condition that they have now. Your physical body is a recordkeeper of your soul. As you are aware, the body does hold memory. It holds the current embodiment of all the lessons and achievements from this incarnation and the past life they correspond most closely with. Although it ages, your body mirrors your choices to grow and evolve. If you are curious about a lifetime that might have caused a current manifestation or condition within your body, focus on that part of your body or condition as you begin to journey. You will begin to see the lifetime that created this imprint in your current self.

At times you might find strong emotions following you from that past life into this one. Acknowledge those emotions and try to understand what memory they were connected to. It can help with processing the emotions so that they can move on. Once again, do not force it if you cannot see the memory. You can also move the emotions along by acknowledging them and then doing things that make you happy.

A practice I learned when I was first starting on this path is to go for a walk and look for a stone that will bear your burdens. When you find it, ask if it would be willing to help you. If you do not feel a negative energy in response to your request, then that stone has agreed to assist you. Breathe whatever sorrows or emotions are unsettling you into the stone. The rock will hold and carry that emotion for you. Fling the stone safely as far away from you as possible. It should release you from the emotion or at least the strongest edges of it.

When you are done studying this lifetime, as always, it is important to say a prayer of gratitude and to release it. I recommend studying only one past lifetime at a time. Working on multiple past lifetimes simultaneously will make you scattered. It can become very confusing in addition to being very draining.

The Sky Kingdom: The Realm of Higher Beings

The Sky Realm is the one with the highest vibration. It is the most beautiful and the vastest. In this world can be found many ascended beings, such as Beings of Light, Star Nations, angelics, and Sky Teachers, who are known in other cultures as *ascended masters*. Since the realm's vibration is so high, it takes training and dedication to be able to maintain focus and stamina there. It would be very much like going into the upper elevations when mountain climbing. The oxygen is markedly scarcer up there than it is in lower elevations. It is important in this practice to take your time as you go into the Sky Kingdom. Just as if you were high in the sky, you would be able to see the whole horizon and a greater picture of how everything interacts, so it is with this kingdom. Here one can journey to see the Dreamweave. A shaman would journey to the Sky Kingdom in order to see and understand the karma of an individual. Here you can see how the lives of an individual and a collective interact with each other to create the Dreamweave. Each and every one of us, and everything in Creation, is a thread in the Dreamweave. Since it is a place so unlike our own here in the Middle Kingdom, those of you who do not feel attachment to this earth nor to this life may find it very tempting to go into the Sky Realm and remain ungrounded upon your return.

Say, for example, that you are trying to understand a past life. In the Lower Realm, you would see the different Powers that had assisted you in that incarnation. In the Middle Kingdom, you would view that life in first person. The Sky Realm shows you that same incarnation from a third-person, panoramic view of how your life fit in with the greater picture by allowing you to observe how your life affected those individuals whose lives you touched. From the Sky Kingdom, you can also see how a past incarnation impacts this current one.

However, because things come from the greater perspective, sometimes even from a grander cosmic perspective, it can be difficult to grasp and properly interpret what you receive here. The same is true with the beings that you find in the Sky

Kingdom. Pretend that there is a problem that you are having in regard to a friendship. Although tremendously helpful with greater issues of soul development, understanding divine law, and karmic Balance, a higher being who has never incarnated, such as an angelic, would be very ill-suited to understanding the nuances of human relations in such situations. You would do much better with an Ancestor spirit because since they have incarnated at least once on earth, they would have a better understanding of what is involved with the subtleties of human communications and interactions. In short, these beings of the higher realms are unparalleled in understanding the bigger picture and the Balance of incarnations within the greater context of the Dreamweave, but they would not be as helpful as one of your Sacred Ancestors, who once lived within the Middle Kingdom, with understanding what it is like to deal with the daily pressures of human existence.

It is good to have allies in the Sky Realm. The beings that inhabit it are highly evolved and can help answer questions and give insights to deeply spiritual or karmic questions. Keep in mind, however, their limitation: although they may understand the workings of the divine and teach you about divine law, they are sorely unable to understand and relate how things work here in this century. Here is when your Guardian would act as your interpreter, to assist you in communicating with this divine being and help you gain insight on how to apply what you've received. Typically, Sky Beings, which also include gods and goddesses, are spirits of great compassion and wisdom. Before you journey, think deeply about not only how you want to grow on your spiritual journey and on this shamanic path but also what your true motives are. The reason is that if you do not know your own Heart, it might be difficult to understand why a specific divine being is aligning itself with you. It is proper to present this to them when you are requesting for one of them to have the compassion and patience to become your teacher. Yes, it is true that you can contact divine beings for information and answers as you need them, but here I am trying to teach you as I have been taught, which is to approach these divine beings with respectful mindfulness and with the intention of creating a lasting relationship that will grow as you grow.

PURIFICATION RITUAL:

HOW TO PREPARE YOURSELF FOR A SACRED RITUAL

When I was taught, I was made to undergo a purification ritual before going on to the Sky Realm for the first time. I recommend that you do the same. It does not need to be complicated. I had to take a purification bath and fast. If you choose to perform these, only do them if you know that you are medically cleared to do so. For the purification bath, draw a bath that is comfortably hot. Poor a half cup of mineral salts into the water, and as you swirl it around so that the salt dissolves, ask Grandmother Ocean to send her energy into the water. The reason we ask her is because as a kind Grandmother, she helps purify us while connecting us with the energy found in the rhythm of her waves. This begins the process of synchronizing us with cycles greater than our own.

Set a timer for twenty minutes. Soak in the water and allow any of the tensions and concerns that have been burdening your Heart and body to go from you into the water. It is not uncommon to see the water turn very inky or cloudy. After twenty minutes, give thanks, drain the water, and shower off like normal. I will give you a friendly warning though: this purification bath is very relaxing! I do not recommend planning any activities after it. If you also choose to fast, only do so if you have consulted with a physician. You do not have to fast for a long period of time; it could be waiting to eat a meal until after you are done. I myself was made to fast for a day. You could also do what is known as a *light fast*. This is when you eat and drink just enough to keep your blood sugars at a safe and constant level but not enough to make you heavy or overly full. You do not need a purification ritual like this after your first journey to the Sky Kingdom.

Journey to the Sky Realm

Since the vibrational rate of the Sky Realm is so different from ours here, I would like to offer you this exercise that might make it a little bit easier for you before you actually go on your shamanic travels. Go outside and look up at the sky. Gaze at it both during the day and at night until you feel one with the sky. It is best if you are able to recline or put a blanket upon the ground so you can lie flat on your back and look upward. As you gaze upward, allow your Heart and mind to be open. Feel the winds as you observe the clouds. Let yourself become one with this element of heaven. At nighttime, behold the twinkle of the stars and the gliding of Grandmother Moon across the sky. The energy of the night air is different from that of the day, but the openness of the sky is universal. Permit yourself to go upon the winds, and, as I like to say sometimes, it may feel as if you are "falling" into the sky. Let yourself be free! Relax and breathe the air deeply. Connect with All Your Relatives of the sky, such as the birds if by day or the bats if by night, as they fly by. Once you feel that you truly have a rapport with the elements of the winds and of the sky, you will be ready to journey. Remember that upon the Good Red Road we always give our gratitude at the beginning and the end of every exercise.

Some of my Medicine Teachers used to say that it is sometimes easier to journey to the Sky Kingdom when listening to wind instruments such as the Native American flute. If you choose wind instruments instead of, or in addition to, a drum, make sure that it is gentle music that is strictly instrumental. In my tradition, we sit facing to the north because it is said that north is the direction that holds the pathway to the sacred realms in the sky. If you do not know your orientation or if it is not possible to face north where you are sitting, that is okay. Connect with your Waterfall and the Fire Within Your Heart. Focus that sacred energy to make stronger the Fire Within Your Heart and remember your connection with the sky. Ask your Guardian spirits to go with you at this time, and then remember and focus on the fact that the purpose of this journey is to introduce yourself and ask a Sky Being to become one of your teachers and allies. Walk into the Sacred Fire into a place within this Middle Kingdom where the view of the sky is uninterrupted. It could even be the place where you were practicing connecting with the heavens.

Open your Heart and open your mind, unite your energy with your Guardian and your Powers, and feel yourself becoming lighter than air. Feel yourself floating upward like smoke or like a feather gently carried upon the winds. Remember that you are safely supported as you go higher and higher. As you ascend, concentrate on the energy within your Heart and mentally voice your request for a sacred Sky Being to speak with you. As you go upon the winds, you will see a sacred mountain. In my tradition, we say the mountain's color is turquoise. Go upon the sacred mountain to give your gratitude.

A protector of the mountain may be waiting to meet you there. Go with your Guardians and with the sacred guide of the mountain. Ask to be taken to a meeting place at the top where you may speak with a Sky Being. Breathe and focus. Let the energy of the Sky Kingdom fill you. You will come upon an overlook. Be seated and be still. Gaze upon the sky and the realms beneath you. Be there in a state of oneness, peace, thankfulness, and humility. If there is a Sky Spirit there, bow your head to show your appreciation and your respect, and introduce yourself. Be open to what this divine being has to say. Feel the energy of this sacred spirit. Ask if this divine being would be willing to be one of your allies as you continue to go about your spiritual growth and life journey. Connect once more with the energy that is the essence of this Sky Spirit. Just as you identify those whom you love by their energy, so will you begin to identify those of the spirit realm who interact with you. Ask this Sky Teacher for a name if you do not already know it or for a way to identify this spirit. Most of the communication may have been through feelings and a sensation of the Fire in Your Heart growing stronger rather than some sort of verbal communication to be understood by your mind. Be at peace in this place, for what is happening is not only a journey to meet your Sky Teacher but also an attunement to be able to Walk more easily within this higher realm. When you are dismissed once again, give thanks for being permitted to be in this divine place. Come back down the path and return at once to the place where you started upon the mountain.

Go with those who Walk with you through the sky and float back down like a leaf landing gently on the Middle Kingdom. Once you are here again, feel the good earth beneath your feet as you go back into the Fire of Your Heart. Breathe deeply. Feel yourself being completely back in your body. Give thanks. Know that this divine being with whom you have connected will now begin to guide you and teach you regardless of if you are in the realms of journeying or here in your everyday life.

Divine Beings

Just as you did your research when you discovered your personal Power Animal, so too must you do your research here. Learn more about the type of being that has chosen to become one of your spiritual mentors. For example, an angelic would have a different disposition from a god or goddess. Understanding what each of them watches over and what their area of knowledge is will help you a great deal. Commonly, a divine being will choose to interact with someone who is in alignment with their purpose or cause. Say, for example, that a Being of Light whose purpose is to help bring peace on earth chooses to speak with you. This being would help bless and enhance the peace within you and around you in addition to teaching you the ways of helping to bring more serenity to this world. It is a sacred exchange. You are gifted with peace, and in return as you live these practices, you help promote the mission of this divine being.

Here is a way of testing to make sure that the being you are talking to is who they claim they are. Let's say there is a spirit claiming to be Archangel Michael. This particular archangel protects us from evil as one of his primary duties. Be wary if there is a being that presents itself as the Archangel Michael and promises you power with the ability to heal—it is not the archangel but a type of spirit called a *Deceiver*.

I would like to take a little time to describe the difference between a Deceiver and a Trickster Spirit. A Deceiver is a type of evil spirit that likes to masquerade as a good spirit. It comes from the Gray Region, which I will talk about later in this book. The more powerful the Deceiver, the higher type of sacred being it can pretend to be. A weak Deceiver might only be able to disguise itself as a Power Animal. A much stronger Deceiver would be able to put on the guise of a Sky Teacher. The real goal of a Deceiver is to ensnare a person so as to drain their energy, disrupt their life, and throw the targeted individual off their spiritual path. They feed on toxic emotions and the Power they steal. The more they take, the stronger they become. On the other hand, *Trickster Spirits* can be a difficult to work with, yet they are benign teachers. Old Man Coyote, who is known to many North American tribes, is said to be one of these teachers. A Trickster Spirit is sent by Creator to guide us when we are stuck or too stubborn to change. A Trickster's strategy would be to persuade or push us to see and do things in new ways during unexpected circumstances. A Trickster Being always promotes growth and serves the Great Mystery.

A sacred being is only able to offer protections, blessings, and wisdom within its jurisdiction! At this early stage, a Sky Being would be satisfied with the exchange if you contemplated the knowledge that was shared with you and, if applicable, properly used it. This is similar to when someone asks you for help or information, and you don't mind if you know that it will be put to good use. So it is with these beautiful sacred spirits.

Build a stronger bond with your Sky Teacher by learning more about this sacred being's preferences. By doing this, you are not worshiping them! The reason I mention this is because it is considered to be a polite courtesy to offer a gift in exchange for wisdom. You are merely offering them a gift in gratitude, much like you would for someone in this world who has helped you. It is no different from offering a friend food and drink in exchange for them helping you paint your house or move. Remember never take more than you can give on this path. Begin to participate in the sacred exchange by doing things to honor them. Some of them may ask for acts of kindness, others may request pleasant music, and others yet find smoke or incense pleasing.

JOURNEY TO SEEK HIGHER COUNSEL

This exercise is to help you to understand how the Sky Realm facilitates seeing things from more of a karmic perspective. Review the journey to the Middle Kingdom, in which you connected with the past life that most impacts this incarnation. Think about another aspect of that lifetime that you would like to understand better. A good question would be what karmic lessons need to be completed and how they impact this lifetime. Since the Sky Kingdom sees things from a greater perspective, you will be able to observe not only your own personal interaction with particular individuals but also the roles they played and why. You will begin to understand how they and the environment plus time period affected your Dreamweave. All these elements have shaped you into who you are today in this incarnation.

Make the usual preparations and bless off. If possible, sit facing north. With a grateful attitude, open your mind and open your Heart, and feel your Waterfall coursing through you. Connect deeply with our Earth Mother. There is an old teaching that says a tree should only grow as high as its roots go deep. Concentrate on deepening the feeling of oneness with the strength of the earth and of your Waterfall. Focus this energy to the Fire in Your Heart. Let this Sacred Fire fill you. Call your Guardians to you. As you journey through the Sacred Fire, you will emerge at a place that is open to the sky. Begin to connect with the sky. Allow yourself to be lifted and those who Walk with you will be your escort.

Call out to the Sky Teacher that offered to be your guide and mentor. Let yourself be drawn to where that sacred being lives. Once you arrive bow in gratitude and begin to express your question not only with words but include your impressions, feelings, and the images in regard to that past life. Be silent and be still. Allow for the Sky Teacher to respond and explain how that past life relates to this one. You will find in the Sky Realm that communication is more than just thoughts and words that are being transmitted to you. It is standard for the energy and knowledge of higher spirits to require a little bit of time for the conscious mind to digest. If there is something that you do not understand, do not hesitate to ask for clarification, as divine beings are patient. If you are ready, this Sky Being of Light and

Love will be more than happy to try to give you more profound insights in a way that you can comprehend.

You might find that you are called back by your Guardians before you feel that you are ready or before you have finished a conversation. This is normal. As I mentioned before, these journeys to the Sky Kingdom take a lot of energy since the vibrational rate is so much different from ours.

Come floating back to the ground and return through the Fire of Your Heart and back into your body. Record what you have experienced. One thing that I must warn you is that time is not linear! You might find it takes a little bit of time to completely grasp what you have been given because events need to unfold before you have the context of the answer that was given you.

As is customary, give thanks and begin to contemplate what you have received.

From the Native American perspective, *life lessons*—or *karma*, as they are called in mainstream culture—are not about dealing with punishment for misdeeds or things overlooked. They are about the Balance of things you have done and what you have yet to learn. For us, karma does not have a connotation of reward or punishment. It really demonstrates how much the soul has mastered and what abilities it has been allowed to carry through to this life. Depending on how much karma has been resolved, some of the souls who agreed to participate in the initial lesson may reincarnate again and again within your soul collective to rejoin you upon your life journeys. Use this knowledge to enrich your understanding and to help you make better choices. Travel to the Sky Realm frequently as your stamina builds to be able to gain a deeper understanding of why things happened and when. The more you journey with humility and respect in this upper world, the stronger your bond with and ability to communicate with these divine beings. Your abilities will become greater because you will become more attuned to these higher vibrations.

When You're Unsure Where to Journey

Especially in the beginning, it is a little confusing when trying to decide which Kingdom you should go to. This is perfectly normal. I encourage you to explore each of the realms frequently so you become more familiar with their unique energies, what you can find there, and who resides there. If you are completely unsure of where you should go, then you can journey into the Fire of Your Heart since this is the place of the Great Spirit within you. Make sure that you have channeled sacred energy from your Waterfall into the Fire Within so that it becomes strong and bright. You can then ask your Guardian to take you to the Kingdom that would help you with the questions that you are working on. However, I do not want this to become a crutch! It is not right to give your Guardians and your guides more work by forcing them to perform an unnecessary task. Here is what you can do to gain confidence: Please write down or at the very least mentally decide which of the spirit worlds that you believe that you should go to. Jot down the reasons you chose it. After that you may go to the Fire of Your Heart and then see if you are right.

As you become more experienced, you will find that this is unnecessary. Going to the Fire of Your Heart is like going to the center of the Medicine Wheel. You have the ability to "see all around you." This is very useful when you are trying to gauge the elements and evaluate which ones are in harmony and which ones are not. This is the perfect place for you to learn how to be still and journey more deeply so that you can commune with the Creator and feel inner peace.

The good news is that there is a failsafe. If you are attempting to go to a realm that would not be appropriate or that you should not be visiting at that time, then your Guardian will make sure to redirect you to where you need to be. It is always a good idea to ask your Guardian why you were redirected so that you may learn to read see the signs for yourself the next time.

The Gray Zone: The Place Outside the Realms

The final realm that I shall mention here is a place that is not a place. It is called the Gray Zone or Gray Region. I only mention this region for the sake of being complete in my duties and responsibilities as a teacher. We do not have a concept of hell, but it is said that the Gray Zone is a place where the Breath of the Great Spirit is not. It is a place that is outside of the Medicine Wheel of Life. It is like a limbo of sorts, a place of lost souls, where evil spirits dwell. It is the location where souls are kept if there has been some major transgression and they need to understand what they have done. Beyond that is the Abyss, from which there is no return.

The good news is your chances of ending up in the Gray Zone are very, very slim. I mention this place only because it is important to learn to recognize it in the very unlikely case you should stumble into it. You will know it because it will be as if you are enclosed by a cold, life-sucking gray fog full of dread. You should call upon your Guardian Spirits to retrieve you immediately and pull you back to safety. There is no reason for a shaman to journey into the Gray Zone.

Throughout this book, when I have said *spirit side*, I am referring to the worlds collectively minus the Gray Zone.

How Good Medicine Can Turn Bad

Since I am on the topic of Deceivers and toxic energy, I would like to touch on how Medicine can go bad. As I had mentioned earlier, Power can be used for good or for evil. There are a few things that you need to be aware of so that you may avoid this happening to you. Be careful not to expose yourself to the sickness of another. The result of trying to heal someone without knowing what you are doing is absorbing their sickness both in physical form and spiritual form into yourself. Unfortunately, over the years I have met several kind healers who gave too much of their own life force and others whose protections were not strong enough for what they took on, and they had literally developed the cancers and diseases of the people whom they cured. If you choose to become a healer of this type, make sure that you go to a master shaman who knows how you may fortify your immunity and properly treat those you are trying to help.

Another common issue can result when trying to take away the toxic energy of another person. If you do not know how to properly handle these poisons, it can create blockages and shut you down spiritually. The bad, chaotic energy can create health issues, mental unrest, and serious instability in all areas of your life.

This next form of Medicine turning on you is, thankfully, exceedingly rare. This is the consequence when someone is trying to cleanse or exorcise a Deceiver or evil spirit that is stronger than they are. With "weaker" evil spirits, the results include being temporarily sick spiritually and physically, increasing to the point of seeing your life and relationships coming undone before your eyes. Very powerful evil spirits, like demons, can possess you.

It is unfortunate that the next way Medicine becomes bad is extremely prevalent in our society. This happens when someone is corrupted by power. This comes when a person is willfully taking more than they should and gives very little in return. Choosing to drain others of time, energy, or resources is parasitic, when one should instead develop their own Power Within. Still others develop a lust for power and for wrongful power over others. This type of corruption is similar to that of someone in authority, such as a politician, whose selfish desires overpower their sense of ethics. Their greed for power and material wealth overshadows doing what is right.

Ultimately, bad Medicine thrown at good people will turn on the practitioner who cast it, destroying and consuming them. If their Heart becomes evil, then when they die, they may be banished to the Gray Region until their soul is cleansed and the Creator releases them.

· SEVEN ·

Interpreting the Journey

One of the most difficult things to do in addition to disciplining yourself to journey is interpreting what you have been given. It can be very difficult because at times the feelings, impressions, and thoughts may not seem to relate to anything obvious. Let me give you methods to help you in this process. When we communicate, whether we are conscious of it or not, we are agreeing upon the use of a language and idioms from a specific country and region in relation to the century from which they are used (e.g., twenty-first-century American English will differ from twentieth-century British English). When you are journeying as a shaman, keep in mind, as I mentioned before, that human beings are the only creatures that use language the way that we do. So that you may have more success, you need to ask your Guardian to work with you in order to create frames of reference. It is these points of reference that allow you to know which interpretations to use, in addition to the context, so you can properly grasp the message that others are trying to relay. Fortunately for you, at times you will also be running into beings of higher consciousness and intelligence on some journeys. These spirits will be able to communicate with you on your level of comprehension using terms you can understand. However, in the vast majority of cases, you are the one who will have to learn how to communicate.

Your Memories as Points of Reference

A point of reference that can be used is your own memories. Our lives are rich with stories from our life experiences that make us who we are. The stories of these recollections can be used as frames of reference that your Guardian can access to help interpret a message that an unfamiliar being may be trying to give you. Say, for example, that you are trying to figure out how to handle a difficult relationship. During your travel to Deeper Earth, a Deer calmly comes to you. The Deer looks at you gently and sends you feelings of warmth and of not being afraid. Although the message on the surface might be sufficient, you might be interested in going further to see what additional advice there might be. At that point, your Guardian will step in to act as an interpreter. In your mind's eye, you get the flash of an image from one of your memories. It was when your best friend needed to be patient with you during a difficult point of your relationship with them. Observe how this friend responded to you and handled the situation that resolved the misunderstanding with the friendship intact. You may be asked to reflect on how the relationship was healed. Pay attention to the lessons and the steps you took to grow during this particular life story. This will help add depth to what the Deer was trying to say to you that your mind could not initially capture.

Use a Memory as a Reference

Here is an exercise that I would like for you to try so that you can become accustomed to your Guardian Spirit using your memories as references. Look back on the journeys that you have done previously. Choose one that you would like to be able to relate to on a personal level. It is important that you have a very clear recollection of this journey that you are asking your Guardian to comment on. When you are done reviewing the journey in detail, be still and allow your Guardian to select one of your memories. Study that memory and see what lessons you have learned from it. What feelings did you have at the time? What type of experience was it? What was the result? Reflect on how these insights from your personal life are parallel to what this journey was trying to have you understand. If your Guardian Spirit does not present a personal memory, then this means that none of your past experiences would be relevant here. You will find that relating the journey to a personal experience you have lived will give it a depth that you would not have noticed otherwise.

Symbols

At times when you ask for clarification, it will not be your own memories that will be used. It could very well be images or symbols from another time and place. In this case it would be good for you to research not only what these symbols have meant historically but also what the norms for that particular time period were. What was considered "normal" two or three hundred years ago would certainly not be considered normal or perhaps even acceptable now. Strive always to understand the connotation of what you have been given in addition to the definition. Doing so guarantees that you will develop a broader vision by being able to accurately decipher information from the messages you receive. This will also give you an idea of how to apply them to your questions or a situation you are looking into.

Since you will be exposed to many different forms of communication, I would like you to do this exercise. Think of a concept and its symbol in your own culture. After that, I want you to research that same concept in different cultures and find the symbol from that culture. Read the history about why they chose that symbol.

Let us explore symbols for good luck. In the United States, one symbol for good luck is the horseshoe, with the points going upward in the shape of the letter U. In Germany, one symbol of good luck is the pig. They even have the expression *Schwein gehabt* which means "having a pig." This expression may have come from the Middle Ages, when pigs represented prosperity and the promise that the family would not go hungry. Today, some Germans exchange marzipan pigs at New Year's Eve for good fortune. So in addition to being a symbol of good luck, the pig embodies prosperity and plenty.

In Chinese culture, one red bat is a symbol of good luck and wards off evil. Five red bats represent the five blessings of long life, wealth, health, love of virtue, and a peaceful death. This is because the word for bat, *fu*, is pronounced the same as the word for good fortune. The word for red, *hong*, is a homophone for the word *vast*. Red is the color of joy. The number five is significant because it represents the five elements of metal, wood, water, fire, and earth, which are regarded as the basis of the whole world. Therefore, depending on the number of bats, this animal represents "vast good fortune" and can symbolize great blessings as well.

In Nordic traditions, the acorn is one of the symbols for good luck. Carrying more than one acorn is said to protect one from pains and illness. This is because it is said that the oak tree is sacred to the strongest Norse god, Thor, who is the god of thunder and lightning. They noticed how the oak tree is extremely strong and also attracts lightning. They also believed Thor would not strike any place that held the seeds of the oak tree, and so the humble acorn is a symbol of good luck—plus it also carries the quality of strength to overcome pain and adversity.

The same symbols can be seen across various cultures but with profoundly different meanings. I always ask my helpers to be specific so that I can get the proper interpretation. A method that has worked for me over the years is to focus on the symbol's visual context. The owl, for example, has several meanings. I'll pick two extremes. It can mean wisdom or death, depending on the cultural context. If the owl comes to me looking like it is inscribed on Greek pottery, then I know that it indicates wisdom. If the owl is presented in the style of an African drawing, then it means death.

So you see, symbols are far more than what they represent on the surface. They are windows into history and culture. Understanding these nuances refines your ability to decipher them.

Finding Your Kin

Each of us has an affinity to certain aspects of the natural world. Since you are learning to Walk the shamanic path upon the Good Red Road by following its practices, you will find that certain families of nature will also have an affinity to you. When this mutual attraction exists, it means that you have been adopted by your kin. Your kin could be the animals, plants and trees, or minerals and crystals. You will find that you intuitively seem to know what they represent and are able to feel their energies very easily. Without much effort, you will be able to talk to them and sense them "talking" back to you.

I will use myself as an example. I am what you would call an animal person. Since I was little, I always felt most comfortable in the company of animals more than people. I have always been able to sense what they needed, and I am able to communicate with them without trying. Animals seek me out no matter where I go. I remember one beautiful spring day when I was walking at a local park with my best friend. We came to the part of the path that went beside a stream, and I saw two fish swimming side by side upstream. I reached out with my thoughts and Heart to warmly greet the fish by sharing my feelings of how happy they made me by seeing them. What my best friend saw next she could not believe. One of the fish actually turned around and swam in front of me, treading water against the current for almost a minute. I was enjoying the company of the fish, the message of contentment, and the feeling of being alive that it was sharing with me. After the fish and I finished our exchange, the fish darted off after her companion.

Although it seems remarkable to my friends that birds and animals are always coming up to me, for me this is normal. If you are a plant and tree person, you will find that you naturally know what they need, love gardening, and have an exceptionally green thumb. Even if there is no wind, the trees will rustle their leaves at you in a pleasing way. If you are a stone and crystal person, it is normal for these minerals to find a way to cross your path or be gifted to you. No matter who your kin are, take the time to not only learn about them as a broad collective but also study the species and types within it. Go further for individuals within a breed or species, for each individual has a unique personality just as we do within our human family.

Here is how you can discover who your kin are. Take time to reflect on which of these families of the natural world you resonate with. Consider if you got a sense of what these beings were feeling or trying to express throughout your lifetime. Have you found that they reached out to you or managed to find their way to you? Pick four members of that family of whose meaning you have no knowledge. Write down the ones that you have chosen and the impressions of the energy that they carry. Research them in reputable sources to confirm if you are correct.

If you have a deep love for crystals or stones, then choose four different types. It is best if you can hold on to the stone in question, but if not, even looking at a picture will work. Connect with the stone with your Heart and then allow your mind to interpret your impressions and record them. You would then look up what spiritual energy they hold and what these crystals have been used for over the centuries. If you find that what you feel consistently matches what the stone is known for, then that means that the Stone Nation is your kin.

Each spiritual pathway is its own "language." It is of key importance that your kin understand which one of these languages you will be using. That way they will know who should appear before you so you can interpret the proper message. Although it might be tedious, the more that you commit the proper interpretations to memory, the more fluent and smooth the communication between you will be. I strongly advise you to become very familiar with one form of interpretation in relation to a spiritual pathway or culture before taking on another. Although it is a tremendous amount of work, I fully encourage you to learn more than one way to interpret what your kin need to tell you. Different spiritual pathways and cultures have nuances that would give your kin a much greater range of expression. You will find in the long run that both of you will be a lot happier! It might feel very mechanical in the beginning, but hang in there. Know that your kin and your helpers are with you every step of the way!

There is another level of relationship with your kin that can only come by journeying and spending time with them. You go from a basic relationship of raw interpretations to one of rich connotations. Take, for example, the dog. It is known throughout the world for its unswerving loyalty, being a protector, and being devoted to greater service. Over the years, while working with the spirit of the Dog, I have noticed a great difference in the way my friend and I relate to it. Whenever she sees the Dog, she knows that something very exciting and positive is about to happen in her life. It is very much like when a dog goes bounding joyfully after finding what it has been tracking for a while. When the Dog appears to me, however, it is to let me know that there is a difficult task at hand, and that I will have strong helpers to see it through to the best possible conclusion.

This is very similar to when you meet someone who develops from mere acquaintance to someone much closer. When you are first becoming someone's friend, it can be a little awkward learning to read each other's signals and habits. As time goes by, you become closer because you have shared common experiences together. Both of you can listen to something as simple as a song and begin to smile at each other. That is because the song reminds both of you of a common experience that made you grow closer. The point of this is that while you are studying a "language," take time to journey and communicate with your kin heart to heart. They, along with your Guardians, will be very enthusiastic about you wanting to get to know them individually and will want to help you grow closer to them.

Ultimately, as you begin to Walk the shamanic Red Road, you will feel a connection to all the families of nature. However, your kin will always be the easiest to "speak" with, while you will be required to work harder to understand what all the other families of nature are trying to tell you.

Developing a Time Sense

This next concept might be a little bit difficult to understand. Time is not linear, although we experience it that way. The reason I mention this is that depending on whom you are speaking with, the insights that will be given to you may not relate to the present moment. They may relate to the past or may be things to watch out for in the future. Because of this, it may be confusing to know when what you've received will be relevant. The first thing you can do is ask your Guardian to tell you directly when the message will be useful. However, you still might find that both of you become frustrated.

Let's talk about developing your sense of time. We all have it. Without looking at a clock, you have an idea of when a few minutes have passed compared to a few hours or a few weeks. I would like to help you go further so that when your Guardian relays when a potential event might happen, you have something more specific to use. I emphasize, however, that the future is ever in motion with very few events set in stone. So you see, trying to get an idea of when something might happen is like attempting to predict the weather. As current circumstances change, so can the outcome of the events and when they might take place.

These two practices will help you create personal time frames of reference that you and your Guardian Spirit agree upon. I recommend that you have more than one way to tell different measurements of time just like you do in everyday life. This will give both you and your Guardians the greatest amount of flexibility in expressing increments of time.

One of the best ways to develop a sense of time is paying attention to what your body is trying to tell you. We all have body clocks. I would like for you to pick a measurement of time that you would like to get a sense of, such as seven minutes. Note the time on the clock or set a timer, and then go do something else. It is important that you are not able to see or hear the clock or timer during this portion of the exercise. When the alarm sounds, stop what you are doing and see how it feels in your body. Do this several times until you feel you are confident that you are able to sense when seven minutes have passed without looking at a clock or timer. Now you are ready to test yourself. Write down the time you are beginning this exercise and go do something else as before. Stop when you sense seven minutes have passed. Only look at the clock or timer when you feel that the time has transpired. How accurate were you? Try this again with different increments of time, such as an hour or a day. Reflect on how long a week feels, a month, one year, two years, ten years. How does your body feel during different types of day? The point of this is that you can actually feel the passage of time instead of only seeing it with your eyes on the calendar or a clock. This is also true when getting a sense of age. What do the energy levels of the different stages of life that you have experienced or observed feel like? Of an infant, a young child, a youth, an adult, or an elder?

Another handy technique is to use the seasons of the year. Here is where your body and your senses can assist you in deciphering a potential time of year. Meditate upon how each season feels. Pay attention to how it affects each of your senses of body, mind, and spirit. How does a season make you feel overall? I like to use the smell of the seasons and the look of nature. If I am given a piece of advice and the distinct look of the trees plus the scent of the frosty bite of winter, I know that the time to use the information will be when this physical Middle Kingdom matches what I saw and smelled in the spirit realm.

The image of a calendar or historical symbols that represent different eras are practical for identifying greater periods of time.

You could even attempt to get an exact month and day if you would like to try to be even more accurate. But realize that this is very, very difficult and requires a tremendous amount of practice. Developing your time sense takes time! Remember to be patient with yourself. You are beginning to learn how to think and move in ways that you perhaps never have before. Just like when you are learning to speak a different language, you only can become better at this with consistent practice as time passes. If you find that you do not understand something initially, instead of pushing yourself to frustration, put it down and come back to it a little bit later. As I said before, since time is not linear, sometimes information is given to you that you do not have a frame of reference for until things develop. This is not fortune-telling! This is like when you give a friend advice for a situation you can foresee the outcome to. What you tell them is meant to guide them to the best possible outcome. This is no different.

Asking Good Questions

The next thing I would like to introduce is what I like to call the *art of the question*. Sloppy questions create broad and even sloppier answers. This is very similar to searching something on the internet: if you put in a very broad topic in hopes of getting a specific answer to a particular question, you will fail miserably. It never ceases to amaze me that so many people feel that they can be very vague about what they are inquiring about and yet are surprised when they receive an answer from their Guardian or helpers that they do not understand.

Here are a few things to consider when crafting a question before going journeying. First, it is imperative that the question is specific enough yet not so specific that it leads the answer. For example, say I am curious about my next step in my spiritual journey. Let me show you a good question versus leading the answer. I could simply ask, "What is my next step so that I may grow on my spiritual journey?" Here the question is specific yet open enough to any possibilities. It allows for a block to be addressed or the suggestion for you to be given a new exercise to help you develop. Perhaps the problem is not even you at all. It could be that the environment is not conducive at this time and you need to wait until the situation changes. Two examples of incorrect questions would be "What is my next step?" and "I am blocked in my spiritual growth because I have trouble journeying. What do I do?" The first question is no good because it is too broad. It could relate to any area of your life or to anyone, for that matter. The second question assumes that the problem is journeying when it could be something else. Therefore, the question is trying to lead the answer, and you run the risk of having tunnel vision instead of being receptive to other possibilities.

Sometimes the things you are inquiring about are too large to fit into a single question. The tip off will be that the answer seems to be vague or like a conversation that wanders aimlessly. If you find that even after asking for clarification, things only become more confusing, then stop and reevaluate your approach. Look at the different elements that you want to know about and make each one of them its own specific question.

Last, upon rare occasion, even if you think you composed the best possible question, you may not get an answer. There are two potential reasons for this. The first one is that you may be asking the wrong question. Ask your Guardian and your helpers to suggest what the appropriate question is. The second one is that you may not be ready for the answer or it may not be timely. Let's say that you journeyed to the Sky Realm to learn about how all of karma works within the entire Dreamweave. In particular, Sky Teachers understand that time has to pass for you to understand the entirety of what you are asking. Those who Walk in harmony will not want to disrupt the Balance of your life by giving you information or insights that you are not yet ready to receive. In this case, request that they share what they feel would serve you best.

Discerning If Something Is a Message

So how can you discern when something is a message or not? If something is a real message rather than your imagination, it will be able to undergo testing and remain intact. Let us say that you have gone on a journey to the Middle Kingdom to feel the energy of the land. While you were there, you met a sacred Grandmother of the Land who greeted you warmly, sat with you, and gave you good counsel. Respectfully inform this benign spirit that you need to test what you are receiving. Intentionally try to superimpose an image of a mouse upon the sacred Grandmother. One of two things will happen: either the image of the mouse will stop the instant you lose concentration, or, more likely, the Grandmother will patiently laugh and nothing will change at all. The equivalent in this world would be you looking at a chair and trying to force it to become an elephant. It might be amusing to someone watching you while you shout and attempt to force this piece of furniture to become an animal, but try as you might, the chair will remain a chair. It is critical to test what you have been given, but do so with a respectful and skeptical yet open mind. Part of showing respect is taking time to digest and demonstrate that you understand and can properly apply what has been shared with you before going back to ask more questions.

Another sign that a message is genuine is that it will keep on presenting itself until you get it right. The universe is an efficient place. The universe will help you if you are having difficulty discerning if what you have received is actually a message or just mind chatter or if you need affirmation that you have interpreted a message properly. The Great Spirit and All Your Relations will send you validations repeatedly and in different ways. Remember that Walking the traditional shamanic path is not merely journeying to the world of the spirits. Affirmations of messages will come to you in both the physical and nonphysical realms simultaneously. You may encounter different people who feel compelled to speak to you, but you are unaware that they are giving you the same bit of advice. You might find the same message being repeated over and over again in dreams.

You may keep stumbling across different signs and symbols, such as number sequences, all pointing to the same thing until you acknowledge the message and interpret it correctly. This is very similar to when you dictate a series of numbers or information, such as an address, to someone. You patiently dictate the information until they can recite the address or number sequence back to you. Do not rush through this! It is more important to ask All Your Relations to kindly repeat what you need to know until you have it down right. Of course, if you find yourself continuously asking the same question over and over because you did not like the answer you received, then you run the risk of having your Guardian and your helpers seen and unseen show you their frustration by not answering at all.

When applicable, research what you have been given. Just like you would when composing a formal dissertation, make sure that you look up more than one reliable reference source before considering something a fact. This should be done when looking into facts about a past life or verifying the details when an entity claims to be a specific divine being.

I would like to interject a point of ethics here. You may delve into your life as much as you want, but you may not delve into the life of another even if you have their consent. At this stage, you do not have enough experience to know where to journey nor to be sure that you are interpreting messages accurately.

Dreams and Visions

There are two other sources that you may gain insight from in the realm of the spirits. They are Big Dreams and Big Visions. Dreams and visions are similar. They usually come unbidden and speak about what you need to know regardless if you had been thinking about a topic or not. Dreams happen when you are asleep. Visions can come from you envisioning things with your mind or daydreaming. Both dreams and visions are generated from within your own emotions and mind. When the dream or vision holds a message from the spirit realm, then we would call it a Big Dream or a Big Vision. It is said that having a Big Vision is dreaming while you are awake.

There is a way to tell whether a dream or vision is simply the construction of your mind or the gateway of the spirit realm. A Big Dream or a Big Vision will feel as real as sitting here in the Middle Kingdom. Your interactions there would make sense and be experienced linearly, and normal conversations are just as they would be in the waking world. A Big Dream or Big Vision will feel very different from a little dream or little vision because you find yourself profoundly moved, and the truth of what you experienced will resonate within your soul. Classic examples of this are seeing a loved one whom you have been mourning or experiencing a visitation from a sacred being, such as an angel, to guide you during times of trouble. Regular dreams or visions will usually be very random and unexpectedly drift from one thing to another. They have no consistency and seem more like a trip through Wonderland since they are fabrications of your subconscious mind.

Usually the Great Spirit will employ Big Dreams and Big Visions as a method of getting your attention when you really need to know something but have not thought to journey on it. Although, this can also be a natural talent, and I am sure that there are several of you that are natural dreamers and visionaries. Ask questions beforehand just as you would with a journey; however, the difference is you will have to wait for the Creator and your helpers to decide when they will respond. Make sure to test Big Dreams and Big Visions just as you would a journey. Here, as with anywhere else in life, the truth will stand and that which is false will fall away.

· EIGHT ·

Journeying with the Elements

Journeying with the elements will help you in a variety of ways. One of them is that you will be able to recognize the energy of each element wherever you run into it. You will also be able to begin to feel when one or more of your elements are out of Balance and get an idea of what needs to be done to restore harmony and well-being. Although what you experience in the Dreamtime will be very vivid, it is very common to have everything suddenly begin to fade away like a dream once you return to this Middle Kingdom. This is why I strongly encourage you to have your journal right next to you and immediately record what you have experienced when you are doing these exercises. I know personally that sometimes there is so much that I cannot seem to write it all down fast enough. At those times, I usually like to record my voice so that I can later transcribe my experiences.

In the Native American traditions I studied, like in many other parts the world, it is said that the world is made up of five elements. The element of spirit consistently remains in the center of the Medicine Wheel, but which element is assigned to each compass point depends on the tribe. To give you an overview, fire is seen as the Breath of the Creator. Air is seen as movement and thought. Water represents the element of Heart. Earth represents the body and environment. Spirit represents soul and transcendence. In order to preserve harmony and health, these five elements need to be maintained in Balance. Doing so ensures that the energy of life flows around you and through you peacefully and with little resistance.

If there is an imbalance of the elements, then there can be sickness and unneeded destructive chaos that run rampant in a person's life. I would like to emphasize, though, that order and chaos are both seen as neutral and necessary forces. As I like to tell people, if you have ever moved or repainted your home, then you know that there is always chaos before new order! If you continue along this path, then you need to further study the interaction of these elements because this is critical to being able to determine what someone or a situation might need in order to restore things as they should be.

In Western thought, if someone is sick or if there is a problem, only that particular symptomatic area is looked at. It is only in very recent history that a more holistic view of wellness and health is being adopted by Western cultures. In the Native American viewpoint, the illness is addressed differently. Say, for example, that someone was overeating due to tremendous stress at work and obsessing about it. The condition is not severe yet but can become so if not addressed. The two elements that are out of Balance are earth, because food is involved and any weight issues are being caused in this case by excessive eating, and air, because his mind is restless and he can't stop thinking about his situation. Western thought would heavily focus on the aspects of his body, which are earth, and his thought process, which is air. Depending on the practitioner, the other elements might not be looked at as closely.

For us, that type of strategy would only be looking at part of the problem. We would first engage the element of water, which is Heart. This element would help us comprehend the deep underlying causes of where this faulty survival habit sprang from. We would then look at energy, which is the element of fire. We would try to understand where he is spending his energy and help him begin to reclaim it so that he could redirect it to something healthier. Finally, we turn to spirit by having him look at the greater perspective of what it is that he wants for himself and for his career, short and long term. It would be very much like adjusting a scale that in the beginning is completely out of Balance because the elements of earth and air are completely tipping the Balance off center. By slowly adding the other elements, the scale becomes more level, and then finally, after the other three missing elements are engaged, we return again to the initial elements that created the imbalance to begin with. We would revisit earth to see how to improve his environment and perhaps suggest a new diet. We would also take another look at air and give him techniques to begin to reframe his situation. This would help him develop a healthier mindset and perspective when working on this health issue

I would like to clarify that if an element is severely out of Balance to the point of causing harm, we would attend to it first and stabilize it before moving on to the others. When you begin to train in this tradition, it is always this way. Balance is a dynamic process. What helps keep things in Balance today might shift tomorrow because circumstances change. The movement of the elements is dynamic within an individual and also within that person's environment.

The way I'm presenting the elements and the directions they are aligned with is in relation to the tribes I learned from. The directions, the colors, and the teachings I share in this chapter are from the Anishinaabe Nation. The animals are strictly of my own choosing because I feel they embody the element and may make it easier for you to connect with the element you are working on. I have created these exercises to assist you in going further in this endeavor. If you study under other tribes or nations, remember that although the universal teachings will be very similar in the manner that they are relayed and in emphasizing which lessons are important to remember, the compass points and associated elements might be very different. Even within a nation there can be variations.

I am describing the elements to help you grow in your spiritual practice. The elements can also be applied to bring greater harmony and order within your environment. I would also like to say that here I am using my kin, which are the animals, to assist us in learning about the elements. I strongly encourage you to go back over these exercises with your kin to discover which of them would help hold the energy and essence of that specific element for you.

The techniques of honoring the elements should be kept the same. You will find that each time you honor the elements, you will receive a different insight in addition to strengthening your connection with the element as time goes on.

Earth: The Element of
Creativity and Building Foundations

It is this element that represents our bodies and our environment. In Native American spirituality, they are inseparable. What you do to your environment will ultimately affect you; what you do to yourself will in the end impact those around you and your environment. The element of earth, when compared to all the others, is the slowest moving but the longest lasting. It teaches us patience and perseverance. Through earth's resistance, we build character and know what we are willing to take a stand for. How incredible it is that what we can feel in our Hearts and envision with our imaginations we can then apply creativity to, manifesting just about anything! Earth's color is red like the rising of the sun. Earth's direction, east, represents infancy when correlated to human age. It is the time in our lives when everything is brand new and we do not yet have a complete understanding of the world that is before us. It represents the season of spring when the land becomes fertile once again. Earth is the element that allows us to complete our karmic lessons and makes us focus on what truly matters.

When this element is in Balance, it is like a pleasant land of rolling hills and golden sun. This sacred element teaches us the importance of giving and receiving equally. The greatest example of this is a potluck meal for a large group of people. It would be too much burden on any one person in both time and money. In the beginning, there is nothing but a bare table. As everybody brings something to share, there is such an abundance of food at the end of the gathering that it actually has to be given away! It is true. When we all give a little, then we all have a lot! This element teaches us the value of thoughtful generosity. If you are willing to be in your body and take care of it, then you will have strong health. If you are willing to be of this world and contribute in a meaningful way, then you will be rewarded with a good environment and a happy life. In a way, the element of earth teaches us in instant "karma." What is inside of you and what you do comes back to you in various manifestations. What we do collectively is reflected back to us in our societies and global environment. When earth is in Balance, we receive nourishment and can see what solid foundations there are to build a life of stability.

When earth is out of Balance, it is like a tremendous earthquake that crushes and destabilizes everything. When this element is out of Balance, then greed becomes a driving factor. Sadly, we see this happening all too often on our own good Earth Mother when so much needless destruction is done for the sake of profit. When this sacred element is out of control, our environment internally and externally becomes increasingly toxic until it can no longer sustain life. This can manifest as weak health or disease in the body as well as instability and conflict in all areas of our lives. When earth is out of Balance, instead of taking time to think about what we are doing, we impulsively jump into things. The result is that there can be long-term harm from those mindless short-term actions.

Power Animal: Monkey

Chattering and smiling at us is the clever Monkey. This Power Animal is honored in many various spiritual pathways. In Hinduism, the god Hanuman appears to be a monkey upon first impression, and the Maya consider monkeys to be the patrons of creative endeavors. Of all the mammals, primates are the closest to us. They live in groups called *troops*. They teach and care for each other and express a wide range of emotions in a manner similar to ours.

When this sacred animal is in Balance, it represents cleverness with the ability to invent that which is new and captivating. The Monkey is family oriented and can easily adapt and take advantage of any situation, whether it be in the wild or within the cities of humankind. This Power Animal shows us the value of focused hands-on creativity and building. In the wild, some primate species build "beds" of branches and leaves as well as tools in order to make their lives easier and more comfortable.

The spirit of the Monkey entertains and is entertaining. Hence, there is the old expression that something funny or mischievous is "monkeyshines." This is an animal that allows all generations to coexist within their troops. And so, this Power Animal sets an example for us that we should also appreciate all our generations from the youngest to the oldest. When the Monkey is out of Balance, it becomes very self-serving and greedy. If the animal feels self-important, then it can become aggressive within its troop and pick fights easily. Whenever it is nervous, it chatters and becomes restless and scattered. It will then jump from thing to thing and does not complete whatever it was doing. This is very much like us when we are undisciplined or afraid.

Journey of Earth

Before you go on this journey to reconnect with the element of earth, I want you to take some time to contemplate in detail the next thing that you want to manifest or achieve. Is there a goal that you are working toward? Remember that this is the element of solid foundations and building upon them. I would ask for you to think about what you wish to accomplish in both the long and short term. What would be the result of you successfully completing this task?

Gather what you need and prepare for your journey. Face east and, if you like, have something red in color to represent this direction. Build the Fire of Your Heart. Deeply connect with your body and the life that is around you. Feel the ground beneath you. As you relax, you will naturally connect more fully with our good Earth Mother as you sit upon her. Focus. Begin to envision the Monkey, with his grin and long arms and legs. Look at his long tail that can grab branches and items. Monkey comes to you with a mischievous smile and a knowing face. He beckons you to follow him, for it is time for you to go for your lesson. Follow Monkey through the trees and feel the mesmerizing motion of the swaying branches. The sensation is almost like rocking gently in a chair. You notice that there are other Monkeys that are also accompanying you. You hear many different kinds of birds squawking in protest as they fly out of your path. You go deeper into the forest until at last you come to a forgotten stone temple. All the Monkeys fall back except one, who is the leader. The leader beckons you into a room within this temple. A hole in the ceiling allows for shafts of sunlight to illuminate the walls that are here. The stone is very worn, but clearly there are the symbols of cultures from around the world and throughout time. The Monkey who led you falls back and gestures for you to sit in the middle of the room to gaze upon the symbols.

Recall to Heart and to mind what it is that you wish to manifest. These are thoughts that you had before you began this journey. If you are working on more than one thing, focus on them one at a time. You will notice that certain symbols get your attention or begin to glow in response to what it is you are seeking to understand. See what symbols stand out. Get up and touch them. What is the energy that you feel coming from that symbol? Open your intuitive senses to understand its meaning. Once you have the answer for one question only, then move on to the other. It is normal to feel as if your head is becoming full of information that you can't quite grasp at the moment and your Heart is brimming from the energy of the symbols and the temple. Do not worry about deciphering things in detail now, for it is more important for you to be in this moment.

Monkey taps you upon the shoulder. If you did not get a chance to get the answers to all your questions, know that you can come here at any time.

It is time to return. Giving thanks to Monkey and to the helpers seen and unseen of the temple, you turn to go back with the troop of Monkeys through the trees. Meet your Guardians and return to the Fire of Your Heart.

Get your journal and draw the symbols quickly, for they may fade like smoke from your memory if you wait too long. Take time to write down everything, for some of the knowledge that you could not grasp consciously while you were in the Dreamtime will begin flowing through you now. Capture everything that you can before it goes away. Sit with what you have been given.

HONOR THE ELEMENT OF EARTH

It is preferable if you sit upon the ground if you are able to and even better if you are outside and can sit with your back up against a tree. If you are inside, then sit next to a plant, or if you do not have a plant, holding a stone or crystal will work as well. Be within your body and spirit. Feel your life force and your own heartbeat. The connection between you and All Your Relations is easy and strong.

If you are outside, feel the life force of the tree you are sitting up against. Permit yourself to become one with the tree and feel the element of earth, how the roots go deep within the earth and draw that energy upward as it stretches into the heavens through its branches and leaves.

If you are inside, perceive the energy within the plant or the stone or crystal that is in your hands. Feel its essence and its connection to earth. Allow the Medicine of this being to connect with your own body. As this energy joins with yours, it will be resonating within you.

Practice equally giving and receiving energy with your breath. Receive as you inhale, give back as you exhale. The better you become at doing this, the more intense the exchange of energy is. In time, this will become second nature. You will receive the blessings of strength, stability, and guidance. While you are here in the state of meditation, begin to contemplate these things. What are you creating in your life right now? Do you have the wisdom, resources, and healthy relationships for the future that you need?

You know you are done when the tree, plant, stone, or crystal begins to lessen what they are giving you. You are politely being dismissed. Be not surprised if you receive some messages. Trees and stones hold much memory and wisdom. They love to share with those people who approach them with humility and a desire to listen and learn. In Native American tradition, we call the stones the *Old Ones* for they are the bones of Earth Mother herself.

Air: The Winds of Thought That Carry Us

The next element I would like to cover is air. It represents thought and process. It is the ability to communicate with all beings seen and unseen. The communications are not limited to merely the written and spoken word but encompass all forms of communication that are possible, such as body language. This element has us focus on our mental structures. It is our mental constructs and outlook that set the tone for how we perceive a situation and can create a predisposition in the way that we would handle it. The direction of air is south, and its color is yellow like the sun at its highest point. The season this direction represents is summer. Chronologically, it represents youth and young adulthood.

When this element is Balanced, it is like a friendly wind. It brings clear thought with honest and open communications. Just as air easily moves and bends around objects when this element is in Balance within us, it gives us the ability to be flexible and to adapt. When we master the lessons of this element, we discover how we can properly pace ourselves when we are working or playing. Air encourages us to be open-minded and helps us laugh at ourselves and at life.

When air is out of Balance, it rages and tears things apart like a roving tornado. It symbolizes scattered thoughts or when the mind becomes so overwhelmed it just shuts down. Miscommunications are common because of narrow-mindedness. As air runs out of control, it manifests as one extreme or the other, such as workaholism or procrastination. When this element is out of Balance, it represents when we are too serious and can overengineer things. Garbled communications and mounting frustrations are the result of not communicating to others in a way that they can comprehend.

Power Animal: Deer

The Power Animal that came to teach us about the element of air is the Deer. The Deer guides us to embrace and unconditionally love all parts of ourselves, both light and shadow. This sacred animal helps us become attuned to the rhythms of nature and our society without becoming lost in them. The Deer shows us about freedom of movement. For many tribes, it is the totem of the shaman and the ability to journey between the worlds. The lessons of this Power Animal teach us how to build bridges between people and instruct us about the Sacred Hoop of giving and receiving equally.

When out of Balance, the Deer represents fearfulness and becoming paralyzed when we see shadows both within ourselves and in the outside world. It is when we have tunnel vision and mindlessly continue on a course of action even if it is self-destructive. We become selective in our memory and in our listening. When the Deer is in this state, it represents anxiety about new people or new situations. It is when we would rather stay stuck within what is familiar even if it is not healthy.

JOURNEY OF AIR

Here we are going to ask the spirit of the Deer to assist us in learning about the element of air. Prepare for your journey as you normally would and sit facing south. If you wish, you may bring something with the color yellow to represent the energy of the south. However, this is optional.

Relax. Kindle and strengthen the Fire of Your Heart. Let it fill you and focus on your breath. Feel your breath going over your breastbone as you breathe. Remain here and continue focusing on this sensation until it is all that exists. Focus on your heartbeat. Its rhythm is like the hoofbeats of a dancing deer. Envision this Power Animal. See the points of his antlers, his sharp hooves, and the color of his fur. Note his clear, dark eyes and his strong yet delicate steps. Feel the spirit of the Deer and ask for this sacred animal to help you.

Follow the Deer to a field and back to his herd. Take time to pay attention to the feeling of the air. Pause to notice how many are in the herd, including the young Deer. Feel the beautiful wind moving around you; it inspires the young Deer to leap joyfully. You can feel the rhythm of their hooves on the ground as they dance. Open your Heart to this energy and feel yourself also wishing to move and dance. Run with the Deer. Let yourself be free like the wind. Become the wind! Revel in the freedom and joy of movement and of being. Free your mind of any doubts and negativity. Enjoy this exciting moment. When the herd stops, it is at the edge of a beautiful forest. Lift your arms to the sky and release any and all tensions that you have in your mind and in your body.

When you are ready, allow the leader of the Deer herd to approach you. See your reflection within his large and beautiful eyes. Receive this Power Animal's blessing. The Deer will breathe upon your Heart and fill it with strength and freedom. Be in this moment. Do not rush it!

When the Deer herd is ready to go, it is time for you to return. Give thanks to this beautiful sacred teacher. Return to the Fire of Your Heart. Breathe deeply and allow for the blessing of the Deer and the lightness of being to run completely through you. Allow it to become integrated into every fiber of your body, mind, and spirit. Once more give thanks and begin to journal what you have experienced.

Honor the Element of Air

Acquire an incense that you find pleasant to smell. If you have asthma or allergies, then you can use cold mist like that from a diffuser that uses water instead. If you are able, go outside and look up at the clouds in the sky. As always, dedicate everything back to the Great Spirit and to All Your Relations by offering the incense or mist to them. Feel the sacred breath of life within you. As you have done previously, focus on the sensation when you inhale and as it goes over your breastbone. Relax. Allow your breathing to naturally become deeper. Open your Heart and feel the air around you. Pay close attention to how it feels on your skin and what smells and sounds there might be riding upon it. Allow yourself to get lost in the sensation of the wind if you are outside or on the plume of smoke or steam if you are inside. Unite your breath with the rhythm of the winds and remain there.

Gaze deeply into the smoke, steam, or the clouds if you are staring up at the heavens. What images or symbols do you see? Do not bother interpreting anything now. Be in the moment. Fill your whole being with the element of air. Once you complete this honoring, give thanks. If you are using incense or smudge, remember to bury the ashes! While you are connecting your breath to this sacred element, contemplate these questions: How does your worldview affect how you interact with life and communicate with others? What is your current mindset?

Water: The Element of the Power Within

We turn now to water, the element of Heart. As stated before, emotions and intuition are important expressions of Heart. It is good to pay attention to how you are feeling and to psychic impressions you receive, but like water, they are only healthy if they flow through you and do not stagnate. This is the place of Knowing, where true, profound transformation begins. It is the element of going into the Great Silence, where you can hear the Voice of the Creator within you, also known as the Voice Within. Manifestations begin here because we attract what we believe, whether we are conscious of it or not. Water's direction is west, and the color is like that of the night sky, which is commonly represented with black or a deep, deep blue. The season this direction represents is autumn. Chronologically, this relates to middle age.

When water is in Balance, it is like a gently flowing river or a calm ocean. It helps you hear the Voice Within. It is the element that allows you to connect heart-to-heart with others so that there can be nonverbal communication, which can be more impactful than words. Water carries you to a place within you where you will discover inner peace. Another gift of the Knowing is an intuitive understanding of divine law, karma, and how the universe around you works. Like the water of a river flowing within its banks, this element will teach you how to create healthy boundaries so that you express and reinforce them so that others will respect them.

When the waters are out of Balance, they become more like a furious ocean or dangerous whitewater rapids. You will sense that your Heart is closed and that you are isolated and lonely. You will feel as if you have no boundaries or that people are constantly violating your boundaries if you have them. When this sacred element is churning like an angry sea, you will experience internal turmoil that can escalate to soul suffering. Toxic emotions will create painful drama and blind chaos that can overwhelm and drown you because everything seems hopeless and personal! When the element of water is crashing out of control, you cannot listen to the Voice of the Creator within you.

Power Animal: Dolphin

The Power Animal that is kind enough to join us is the Dolphin. This animal is seen in many cultures as a protector and a good omen. It has been recorded from centuries ago up to this current day that the dolphin has the compassion to save other species, such as human swimmers. When this Medicine is in Balance, it opens and deepens our connection of Heart with ourselves and All Our Relations and can help us navigate our sea of emotions. This inquisitive animal reminds us to keep on playing and learning new things throughout our lives. The dolphin lives in pods and is the perfect instructor regarding the power of cooperation and community. Since this sacred animal has heightened senses and intelligence, it can assist you in learning to read the currents of energy and the trends of a situation while using your intuitive abilities.

When the Dolphin is out of Balance, it becomes irresponsible and childish. Its intelligence is used for manipulation and is divisive. This Medicine, when out of control, can manifest itself as insensitivity toward others in words and action. In this mode, the Dolphin is lazy and becomes petulant if asked to do anything at all.

JOURNEY OF WATER

It is time now to dive into the oceans with the Dolphins. Prepare for your journey and sit facing the west. If you wish to represent this sacred direction, you have the option of bringing something that is black or at least very deep blue in color. Begin your Waterfall; concentrate and completely surrender to the flow of this divine energy flowing through you and around you. Send this energy into the Fire of Your Heart. While you are in this meditative space, pay attention to how you truly feel very deep inside your own Heart. What emotions are you experiencing in different areas of your life?

When you are ready, focus and envision the Dolphins in the ocean. You see swift movements and fins breaking the surface of the water. You hear their whistles and clicks as they call to you. Go into the ocean and feel the waves. Know that you are safe, for the Dolphins are all around you. They invite you to swim with them; if permitted, you may ride one. If you allow yourself to connect fully with the energy of this sacred Power

Animal, you might shape-shift into a dolphin. The tides carry you and feel very soothing. The Dolphins' sleek bodies are graceful, and they invite you to leap playfully as they do in the ocean. As you go racing through the waves with the Dolphins, release your sorrows and any toxic energy that you have. The shining sun burns this energy off and restores the ocean to its beautiful, pristine state. The Dolphins guide you to a cove that holds a magnificent crystal glowing brightly with divine Power. Experience its color, energy, and light. When you feel that you have permission, gently take the crystal in your hands and touch it to your Heart.

Let go! Permit yourself to be open to receive the energy of this crystal, touch it, and let it suffuse every part of you. Be receptive to the messages and blessings that this crystal is giving to you. You will know when the crystal wishes to be returned to its place within the cove. With respect and gratitude, return it to its place. The pod of Dolphins is joyfully whistling and jumping. It is time to return. Once more go into the water and enjoy the sensation of being with them through the rolling waves.

Back upon the shore, you rejoin your Guardians to return to the Fire of Your Heart. Take a moment to enjoy the sensations and bask in the energy that is now throughout you. Breathe deeply and relax. You do not need to rush here. When you are ready, open your eyes, and be in your Heart. Remember to record what you have experienced.

HONOR THE ELEMENT OF WATER

Most people find water to be the easiest of the elements to connect with. Get a bowl that has no decorations on the inside.

A darker colored bowl will make this exercise easier but is not critical for success. If you are able to be outside and work with moving water like the sea or a river, that is even better. Fill the bowl almost to the top with clean, clear water. If you are outside, see the reflection of the sky upon the surface the water. If you are inside, use soft light, and do not have the light source directly reflected on the water.

Sit quietly and concentrate on your breathing. Gaze with *soft eyes*. This means that you allow your gaze to become unfocused, or as if you are gazing at a depth that is twice as deep, beyond the bottom of the bowl. If you are outside, soften your gaze upon the movement of the water or the ocean waves. Focus on your heartbeat and connect it with the energy and, if you are outside, the rhythm of the water. Let your mind be open and trust your feelings. Become one with this divine element. Feel the calmness of the water and let it touch you to calm the waters of your soul. Allow this sacred element to cleanse you and energize you. If you begin to see images on the surface of the water or sense energies, do not interpret or engage them. Let them flow by. Remember that you are here to Balance the element of water within you.

When you are connecting with this sacred element, it would be good to contemplate these three questions: What do you really believe in your Heart about yourself? Does life support you? What beliefs need to be let go and what new beliefs need to be brought in? Once you are done, give thanks to all your helpers seen and unseen. Give the water that is in the bowl back to Earth Mother. You can do this by watering your plants or by pouring the water outside on the dirt. It should never be thrown down the drain, as that would be very disrespectful. Record what you have experienced.

Fire: The Breath of the Creator Within Us

Fire is the Breath and Energy of the Great Mystery. It represents the life spark. Out of all the elements, fire is most like a living being. It starts off as a small and weak ember that needs to be nurtured or it can easily die. It needs to be constantly fed and be given enough nourishment of both fuel and air in order to grow. As it becomes larger, fire requires more "food" in order to sustain itself. Fire can have offspring in the form of other flames that also grow and mature. Ultimately, if fire is not maintained and if it is not given proper shelter, it can age and die. Of the directions, this is the compass point of north. Its color is white like the winter sun, and the season it represents is winter. Chronologically, it represents old age. I joke that it is a uniting factor because it does not matter what ethnicity you come from—as we age, we all get "snow on our mountaintops."

This element teaches us that we must pursue our passions responsibly. Just as fire can help us see in a dark room, Sacred Fire helps illuminate the darkness within our souls and helps us understand our shadows. When fire is properly maintained, it can warm us, protect us, and cook our food so it is safe to ingest. When your Sacred Fire is properly cultivated, it can help protect you from the darkness of the mind and toxicity in the environment. It is able to give you the wisdom to see things from a greater perspective so that hard concepts are broken down and you can easily integrate them.

When fire is out of control, it becomes a wildfire that does not differentiate what it chooses to consume and destroy. It obliterates everything in its path. When a person's Sacred Fire rages out of control, it will ultimately destroy their life by "burning" the people around them and can also destroy their work life by putting too much energy in the wrong places. When fire turns dark, it will create bad Medicine by wanting to wrongfully take energy from others, and it can also manifest itself in the form of all-consuming jealousies and a wrongful sense of superiority. Eventually, just like a physical fire, a person will suffer from burnout.

Power Animal: Jaguar

The Power Animal that I ask to assist us is the Jaguar. The Jaguar is very prevalent in spiritual traditions, especially in the southern points of North America, in Central America, and in South America. This animal is very strong and is at the top of the food chain where it is found. The Jaguar represents personal Power and building self-confidence. When this Medicine is in Balance, this Power Animal teaches us how to engage and temper the gifts that we have in order to *create* our reality. This big cat symbolizes leadership and overcoming obstacles through well-thought-out action.

When out of Balance, the Jaguar can bring direct conflict through contests for dominance and of will. It can become drunk with its own Power and be given to excess. Leadership becomes arrogant tyranny. Might makes right, and there is no regard for who or what is destroyed in the process. Perseverance becomes blind stubbornness.

JOURNEY OF FIRE

On this journey, we're going to ask the Jaguar to show you and to strengthen the qualities of the fire within you. I ask you to sit facing to the north. If you like, you can have something white in your sacred space to represent this direction, but this is optional. Call your Guardians to you. Feel the Fire of Your Heart. Focus and envision a Jaguar. Ask the Jaguar to come to you. Feel the strength of this powerful animal. See her sleek movements and the fire in her eyes. Connect with the Jaguar.

Ask her to take you to see the Sacred Fire. In this place, there will be a ceremonial fire ring made of white stones. This fire is a reflection of the Fire within your own soul. Meditate and feel it. Note its color. Inquire what can be done to strengthen your fire. Be open and listen to the wisdom she gives you. Feel the strength of this big cat and ask her to lend some of her energy to your fire. If you find that the flames are smoky, dark, or fluttering weakly, that means that you have blockages and are allowing toxic people and energies to influence you too strongly in your life. If this is the case, then ask the Jaguar to use her sacred breath to cleanse the flames. Let her teach you how to feed your Sacred Fire properly. Thank the spirit of the Jaguar for all that she has shared with you.

Gently return with your Guardians back to the Fire of Your Heart. Once you are fully back, start reflecting on what you have been given. Make sure to practice what you have been shown so that your soul's Fire may remain in Balance.

Honor the Element of Fire

Get a candle. It does not have to be large, but it should be no smaller than a votive candle. If you can get one that is white, then that is preferable. Dedicate the candle to the Creator and to All That Is. Once you have done this, then the candle should only be used for your shamanic practices.

If you are able to be outside, you can use a bonfire instead of a candle. An offering of smudge and tobacco will need to be thrown into the fire as you dedicate it to this spiritual purpose. This particular fire may not be used for anything else after this point. When you are done with this exercise, thoroughly extinguish the fire as normal to protect the environment.

Face to the north. Light your candle and begin to gaze at the flames. Relax. Allow for yourself to get lost in the movement of this little fire. Feel the Fire Within, feel the energy of your own spirit. Breathe deeply. Open your Heart and feel the connection to the candle flame. The flame represents the Breath and Fire of the Great Spirit. Be open. Go deeper. Allow the Fire Within to connect with the fire before you. Be in this moment completely. While you are communing with this element, begin contemplating these questions: How are you using your energy? What is it creating in your life? What are you feeding the Sacred Fire Within You? Give thanks. Snuff out the candle. With an open Heart and mind, sit and reflect on the answers that you have received.

I know it goes without saying, but I shall say it anyway: *never* leave a lit candle unattended! In this spiritual practice, to extinguish it, snuff it out. *Never* blow out a sacred flame.

Spirit: The Element of the Great Spirit That Lives Within Us

We have reached the last element, which is spirit. This is the element within us that channels the Breath of the Great Spirit and unites us with the Creator. This element is the most Powerful of all of them and can be the most elusive to understand. Spirit is our soul. Connecting here gives us the capacity to see the big picture and the essence of any situation or relationship. Cultivating the element of spirit will help you evolve and go further on your spiritual journey. This is the element of transcendence and is not confined by time or space. The direction that it has is the center. Since this is the aspect of us that is a part of the Creator, it does not know limitations. Several tribes would place a star that pointed to the Four Directions in the center of the Medicine Wheel. So, because of this, you may use your favorite color, for all colors are the colors of spirit. This element allows us to understand karma and comprehend intuitively those things that go beyond logic and the five physical senses. With the element of spirit, we can gain insight to what our soul agreements were before we incarnated. It is through here that we are able to go beyond our own selves and connect with All Our Relations.

When in Balance, the element of spirit allows us to commune directly with the Creator. Here we can sit with our sacred selves. This is the element that instinctively tells us how our choices impact ourselves and others so that we can make Balanced decisions. A Balanced decision is one that takes into account equally your personal needs and the needs of the many. This is the element of enlightenment and unity. When in Balance, it is like a bright shining star that brings life and light during the darkest times of our lives.

When it is out of Balance, then the element of spirit within us is more like a black hole. It brings isolation and despair. You can feel as if you are locked strictly into this physical world. Instead of unity, there is a disconnection and disassociation with life. When spirit is out of Balance, there is a block to the Breath of the Great Spirit, and you will be in a constant state of exhaustion. It will seem as if life does not support you and all there is is suffering no matter what you do. Disconnection from this element can also come when you do not own your actions and words.

Power Animal: Eagle

The bird that comes soaring in to guide us to connect with the element of spirit is the majestic Eagle. The Eagle has been a symbol of Power and leadership throughout the centuries. In Native American spirituality, the Eagle is the great messenger to the Creator. It is said to fly higher than any other bird, and it has the capacity to see from great distances as well as being able to focus on small details. When this bird is in Balance, it teaches us about the Balance between the needs of the self and the needs of the community. Eagle likes order and structure. It will show you how to use these properly to preserve and be the vehicle of what you are trying to create. Eagle is the perfect instructor to teach us how to use our oversight of a situation plus insight, which identify the details of a situation, together to manifest the best possible outcome. It is taught that Eagle flies so high that it is able to carry our prayers and strengthen our connection with the Great Spirit. Eagle has the qualities of both justice and mercy. It has the spiritual ability of translating divine messages and law into simple concepts and practices that we can follow.

When the Eagle is out of Balance, it abuses Power because it arrogantly believes that it is above the law and that it is the ultimate authority. It can be very unfair, favoring those it likes to the detriment of others. Eagle can be extremely overprotective of what it believes be true or thinks is important, regardless if that is actually true or not. When the Eagle is in this way, it is negatively judgmental and critical of anyone who does not conform to its views. Eagle can be relentless in achieving its goals no matter what the price, including the wrongful idea that might makes right. Instead of supporting peace and unity, this sacred animal will be quick to fight with total disregard for the final results or how high the price.

JOURNEY OF SPIRIT

The point of this journey is not to answer questions. It is to learn how to go to the place of spirit within you. Engage this element to develop a deeper sense of oneness with the Creator and with All That Is. This journey is a way of connecting with your own soul. You may sit in any direction that you are called to, and if you wish to have a representation of this element by using your favorite color, you are welcome to do so. The color that you choose can change each time you do this journey since you may be working on different aspects of yourself and of your life. Complete your preparations to journey and kindle the Fire of Your Heart. Concentrate on it so that it becomes bright and strong. Pay attention to what it feels like, the color of it (if it has one), and how strong it is.

Concentrate on your desire to become more connected to the Creator and All That Is. Focus and breathe. Envision Eagle with his sharp eyes that can see right through you. See the details of this bird's powerful wings and sharp talons. See it soaring and coming toward you. With a sharp cry, the Eagle calls you to follow him into the sky. Deep within you, something responds and wishes to fly free with this Power Animal. It is your soul. Concentrate on your desire to become more connected to oneness.

Focus. A feeling of jubilation moves through you as you spiral ever higher with the sacred bird. You can feel your own wings. See the vastness of the heavens above you. See the beauty of Earth Mother below you. Open your wings and soar upon the winds that are the Breath of the Great Spirit. Feel the element of spirit within you. It shines like a bright star within your Heart. See how it responds to being here in the Dreamtime.

You follow the Eagle even higher and see a bright light that is stronger than the sun, but it does not burn you. It is the Light of the Creator. Let the rays of light from the small star that is your soul within you touch the greater light. If you find that it is too intense, then it is okay to circle at a level where you are comfortable. Let yourself be open, for there will be so much that you will wish to express that has no words! Allow yourself to be in this radiance, which is made of divine love, profound wisdom, and infinite compassion. Do not be surprised if, when you try to see yourself, you have become pure light. After all, we are merely spirits having a human experience.

You will know that it is time to return because you will feel completely satiated but not uncomfortably so. The Eagle whistles and calls you back. Follow this sacred bird back to the Fire of Your Heart. He gives you a blessing by fanning you with his wings. This helps secure the blessing of your journey into your body. Express the deep gratitude that is in you and fully return into your body. It might take you a little bit to be able to be completely back, so take your time and do not be in a rush to stand up. It is also very common that when you are working on the element of spirit, Sacred Ancestors or Sky Teachers will join you. If this is the case, then feel honored and take the time that they request to "sit" with them. Usually, they will gift you with advice so that you can learn how to integrate and better harness the energy of spirit. Spirit is the element that you can journey with to take a look at your other elements to see which ones need to be put back into alignment if you are unsure.

If Sacred Ancestors and Sky Teachers join you, spend time with them. You are in the place of eternity. Let yourself feel healed if you are carrying sorrows; this is the place to feel what divine and Balanced Power should feel like.

Honor the Element of Spirit

Spirit is the easiest to honor of all. Since this element is of the Great Spirit, who is in all things and beyond all things, what you do in the name of the One and of the many is a way of honoring this element. Take time to meditate and pray. Acts of kindness and compassion for the greater good that are so needed in this world, so long as they come from a place of authenticity, will feed your soul, Balance the element of spirit within you, and help you evolve. Simple things like drumming, chanting, and playing a musical instrument are ways of expressing joy that do not have to always use words. Another way would be to sit peacefully and just be.

When you are doing this, it is good to contemplate these questions: Do you know your greater purpose and are you willing to live it? Are you living authentically? Let your mind be silent. Allow your Heart and the element of spirit to respond. Ask that you be shown what you can do to grow in alignment with your greater purpose and with becoming who you were meant to be.

NINE

Crafting Shamanic Tools

Now that you know how to safely journey, have identified your personal Medicine, and have begun to interpret what your Guardians are trying to tell you, it is time to harness your creative abilities. Tapping into your creativity is a wonderful way to develop your personal Power and gain confidence and self-expression. A crafted sacred item also acts as a bridge between the spirit world and the physical world. It will help you directly channel Power that the object holds. For now, I will gently remind you that you are to create items only for yourself and not for another person.

Everyday Items as Medicine

Not all shamanic tools are drums and rattles. If you engage in a specific activity consistently for the greater good or the purpose of bringing good Medicine to the world, you can also turn the activity's tools into sacred objects. Be aware that once you do this, these items should be strictly used for this purpose!

One of my students crafts beautiful wooden items that have been "kissed by lightning" through channeling electricity. He has dedicated his workshop, power tools, and all the hand tools that he uses for this purpose back to Creator and bringing positive energy into this world. I have yet another student who is a drum maker and has done the same with all the tools and materials for crafting musical instruments for spiritual work. And I can think of still others, a family, who are very deeply connected with the Medicine of the plants and trees. They love to cultivate all kinds of vegetation. They have dedicated the soil, the plants, and all the items necessary to grow healthy plants back to Creator. They have noticed that the plants thrive vigorously and people respond positively because of the good Medicine.

First Medicine Pouch: Your Ready Bag

I would like to share with you an item that would be good for you to have. One of my teachers introduced me to this practice long ago, and I still follow it today. It is a type of Medicine bag that I have nicknamed a *ready bag*. The reason I call it a ready bag is because it is filled with things that at a moment's notice I could give as proper offerings of gratitude to the spirits. It also can act as a portable personal altar of sorts, so you may meditate and connect more deeply with your Guardians no matter where you are.

This Medicine pouch does not have to be big. Mine is small enough to fit into the side pocket of my drum bag. It is the quality of the offerings that counts, not the quantity! The bag should be made of a natural material such as leather or fabric. I know of several folks who made a small box made of wood. Within should be the accoutrements for smudging, such as a small bowl or shell, smudge, matches or a lighter, and a feather. Other offerings can be added, such as cornmeal and tobacco. You should also have an offering bowl and crystals or fetishes that honor your spiritual helpers. You may also personalize it by adding other crystals and items that have meaning and help you connect more deeply with your own Medicine.

CREATE A SHAMANIC TOOL FOR YOUR PRACTICE

Here is a method for creating a shamanic tool. There are some things you need to think about before you get started. An important one for you to reflect on is what purpose the tool is going to fulfill. Is this item going to be dedicated to a specific sacred spirit? What Medicine Power do you want it to hold? What exactly is the item you are crafting? After that, choose and gather the items, tools, elements, and any embellishments that you will use to create the item. You will also need to have an offering of gratitude that you will give back to the land. It can be cornmeal, natural tobacco, or a gift of beauty, such as a pretty stone or an honoring chant that you sing. Make sure that the workspace and whatever you selected is blessed in addition to yourself. Think carefully about which kingdom you would go to in order to bring back the Power to awaken the item.

Place everything in front of you and prepare to journey. Walk into the Fire of Your Heart. Ask your Guardians to escort you to the kingdom that you will need to go to. Once you are there, focus with your Heart and your mind on what you are crafting and ask that an energy or spirit who would be willing to assist you make itself known. When it appears, give thanks for this kindness and present the offering of gratitude. Allow yourself to feel and connect with the sacred Power that is being gifted to you. You will know that you have received enough when either you are dismissed or you feel as if your Heart is full. Begin journeying back to carry this Medicine through the Fire of Your Heart. Remember, you are only to bring back the Power and *not a spirit!*

Breathe the energy into the main body of the item that you are going to build. Say, for example, I am making a prayer feather. I would breathe the Medicine into the feather and anything else I have decided for sure is going to be a part of the finished product. While remaining connected to this energy, permit your creativity to flow through you. Allow the images, colors, and decorations to be an expression of what you have experienced in the spirit realm. Everything that you put upon your sacred tool has to have meaning! When you feel that you have completed it, focus and release the last of the energy into your creation. You are using the Breath of the Creator that is within you to awaken the object because that is what turns it into a sacred shamanic tool. Seal the Medicine by bathing your sacred item in the smoke of smudge.

If you find that you cannot finish crafting the object in one sitting, then cover your work in progress with a red cloth made of natural fabric. This includes all the tools and items that you are using. When you return, with the help of your Guardians, connect with the images and energies on the spirit side that came to you when you first journeyed. Channel this sacred energy until you are finished.

Once an object becomes sacred, it must be cared for in a special manner. In my tradition, you should *never* touch the Medicine of another person unless they give you explicit permission to do so! You should follow the same rules for your own sacred tools. Once you are done using your shamanic item, it should be stored in a special place, such as your personal sanctuary. I will describe how to create a sanctuary in chapter 11. The reason we use the color red is because it represents the Breath and Fire of the Great Mystery. Wrapping your sacred tools insulates them from random energies in addition to keeping them physically protected.

It is important that whatever you have created you use frequently. Your tools will hold the memory and energy of your lessons. The more you use them, the stronger the Power within them becomes! Sometimes, a shamanic tool can develop a personality. For example, I have two drums. My shield drum bears the symbol of my name. She is used for calling everyone to prayer, to hear the teachings, or to ceremonies. She is a diva and does not like being touched by anyone except me. My other drum is a sweat lodge drum. I use this drum for community ritual, and he has earned the nickname *Smiley*. This is because he loves everyone and enjoys being played by anyone. The joy of the spirits can be felt with every drumbeat when Smiley is used for ceremony.

Acquiring a Drum

Since we are on the subject of drums and rattles, I figured I should address that here. After you have been Walking on this path for a bit, there will come a time when you will want your own drum or rattle. I frequently get asked several questions, so I would like to answer them here. Although it does make it more powerful and personal, you do not need to make the drum yourself. If you come across an instructor who knows how to make traditional Native American drums, please take advantage of it! This is a dying art and it should be preserved. I have been told by many who have crafted their own drums that there is nothing like connecting with its spirit in helping it be "born" into the world.

I know that there are many of you who would not want to use the hide of any animal. So no, your drum does not need to be made of animal skin. There are many great drums out there that have synthetic drumheads and have a great sound. I also get asked a lot if it needs to be a specific type of drum. I would say not really, but it would not be an African drum such as a djembe or Cuban drum such as bongos. A drum that you can easily hold in one hand will serve you best, and traditionally we use single head beaters only.

What really counts is the "voice" of the drum. The drum represents the heartbeat of our beautiful Earth Mother. As you know, each drum has a different pitch. I prefer drums that have a deeper call, and I know there are people who prefer them to have a higher sound. You will know that the drum tone is correct because when it is played, you will feel it connect deeply with your Heart, and it will move through you in a way that gives you joy.

Whatever type of drum you get, regardless of what it is made out of, it is important to ask how to care for it. Failing to do so can cause the drum's rim to crack or the drumhead to split. Just like any other shamanic item that you have, you need to journey to find the Medicine for your drum. It is critical that you connect with your instrument and hold it throughout the whole journey. If you are able to beat the drum as you do this journey, it will be much easier to find its Medicine and make the connection between the spirit realm and the physical body of the drum more Powerful. However, if you are unable to do this, it will still work if you have someone else beating a different drum while you hold your own. Once you know the Medicine that your drum is supposed to have, breathe it into the head of your drum.

Whatever you paint upon the face of the drum will be the prayer and the energy that will connect it between the worlds every single time that drum is beaten. Paint and decorate the drum yourself if you can, but if you are unable to, then you can contract an artist. You need to be *extremely* specific about the image if you have someone else painting it. I personally recommend interviewing several artists and seeing their portfolios to make sure that their style of art will accurately capture the spirit of the Medicine that you want on your instrument. You only have one chance because once the image is on your drum, it is never coming off. Sometimes a drum will choose to have its face completely painted, and others prefer to chronicle its journey with you over time. There is no one right way.

In order for a drum to be fully connected and act as your helper by being a bridge between the worlds, it needs to be awakened. In this tradition you need to approach someone who is Medicine or a spirit person, such as a shaman or a spiritual leader of the tribe. You would need to offer them a gift of tobacco at the very least, and if you wish to go the extra mile, perhaps you can gift them something else as well. However, I will give you a way of beginning to bless your drum since it may not be easy for you to find a traditional Native American spiritual teacher to perform the ceremony for you.

Sit and consider the energy and prayers that you would like your drum to carry. The first song that is sung is important because from the first drumbeat until the end of that drum's days, the meaning of the song will be the purpose of that instrument as it moves through the worlds. My sweat lodge drum's first song was an intertribal Medicine Wheel chant because I play it for ceremonies that welcome all people who want to come together to pray. Smiley will only serve in that capacity. The first song attunes the drum. Once you have decided on which traditional chant or song you will sing to bless the drum, move it in a clockwise, circular motion four times through the smoke of smudge. Dedicate the drum to the Great Spirit and any other helping spirits that have shown themselves. You may be inspired to honor them by having their images painted upon your drum. Feel the joy as you beat your drum and sing the song, which is its birth song. Once you are done, close the ceremony by once again moving the drum four times in a clockwise, circular motion through the smoke of smudge. Your drum from this point forward will now serve the Creator and All Your Relations and act as your "horse" that you ride upon your shamanic travels.

The procedure for rattles and flutes is much the same as for drums. Some people prefer their flutes to be made from man-made materials because they do not warp or crack easily in addition to being easier to transport. I know a professional flute maker who crafts them out of PVC pipes of various diameters for these reasons.

· TEN ·

Tying It All Together

Once you begin to develop a strong baseline of proficiency, it is the perfect time to learn how to use these traditional shamanic skills in everyday life. These newfound abilities can help you maintain your health and wellness in addition to giving you the insight to solve problems and guidance on the decisions that impact your life and the lives of your loved ones. Remember that Native American shamanic practice is meant to be a method that uses the intuitive wisdom of your Heart and the analytical power of your mind equally.

If events in your life are creating stressful energy more often than normal, you can release it by increasing the Power flowing through your Waterfall. See if that is enough. Usually, situations are a bit more complex than just that.

I will now walk you through the steps of how you can use all the different skills taught in the book so far to guide you through situations that come up for you. The first step, as you know, is to develop the proper questions and get an overall look at the situation that you are trying to get answers for. Analyze it with your mind as well as sense with your Heart what other energies are attached to it. Factor in your emotions and your mental outlook because they will influence you.

Summary for Tying All the Lessons You've Learned in This Book Together and How to Apply Them

Here is an outline of the steps for you. You may not necessarily need to utilize all of them, for every situation, but this should give you an idea of how you can put the hours of practice and of honing your skills to good use.

1. Look at the question and the situation surrounding it and analyze it.
2. What is the desired outcome?
3. Is the desired outcome in Balance? Why or why not?
4. Find out what strategies to use by visiting with your kin.
5. Find out which energies are most needed by touching base with the five elements.
6. Is there further guidance from a greater perspective that is needed? If so, journey to the Sky Realm and speak to one of the higher beings. Remember that they will also tell you what you have to release in addition to what you need to do.
7. Sit with all the information and energy that you have gathered in the realm of spirit. Combine it with your own intellect so that it can be formulated into practical actions in this twenty-first-century world.

Example One: Looking for a New Job

Say, for example, that I am looking to start a new job. The current job that I have is not bad, but I am finding it very limiting. I would like to see how else I can grow my career. Analyzing the situation, I notice that the job market has many opportunities for me now. I can safely look for a new job since I am under no pressure. The next step is to decide what my desired outcome is. In this particular case, it would be to end up with a new job that offers me better pay, includes benefits, and allows me to expand my skills so I can grow my career. It is important to be clear about what your desired outcome is because that alone can give you clarity about whether a situation is worth engaging or not. But since what we desire is not always the best for us or timely, the third question I should ask is if the desired outcome is in Balance and for my greater good. In addition to logically investigating why this may or may not be in my best interest, I then begin the journey with my Guardians to the Fire of My Heart. In this space, I pose the same questions, feeling which of my internal energies may influence the outcome. I welcome guiding spirit beings that come to answer my question. Say, for example, that in this case I go to the Fire of My Heart and the one who comes to be with me is my grandfather, who in life always watched out for me. He says that a new job would be good for me because the timing is right, and it would encourage me to grow as a person as well as benefit my family.

Knowing that this situation is a good one and that I should pursue it, the next part I would need to look at is strategy. The next step is to pose the question to my kin. I journey to the Realm of Deeper Earth to see which Power Animals would come to assist me. I also observe their behavior, as that begins to give me insight to the strategies that I should use. In this example, I go journeying to the Lower Kingdom. Of my kin appears a Cougar, who makes sure I see her marking her territory after roaming it to see that all is in order. As I go further along, I see Rabbit, busily digging a burrow alongside a river to make a new home and advising me to do the same. At the river, three female Beavers stop their labors on their dam, and they come to greet me and welcome me as one of their own. They want me to help them continue building the dam.

My Guardians come to escort me back. I thank each of my kin in turn for approaching me and showing me what I need to know. The message that I received from the Cougar is that I must show my ability to lead and to manage the greater responsibilities that will be given to me. The burrowing Rabbit shows me that when I seek my new job, it is like looking for a new home that I can settle in. The Rabbit teaches us that we forespeak our own futures and that our attitudes influence the self-fulfilling prophecies that we create. The three Beavers are significant in that Beavers represent a work culture of cooperation and camaraderie. Since the Beavers were female, I know that I am to look for a company whose leaders are women. To these women, a candidate must be like a member of a family to be accepted as a perfect fit for their company.

Now that I have the strategy, it is good for me to know which energy is most needed for success. This is where the elements come in. Since I am not too sure which of the elements would be needed, I journey to the spirit side. I ask the Eagle to indicate to me and lead me to the direction of the elements that are necessary for success. The Eagle guides me to an ocean shore where there is a fire burning. She lands with me and gives me a feather from her own wing. Eagle speaks to me and advises me to take a careful look at how this new job will impact not only me but those whom I love. Here I gratefully receive the energy of water, fire, and spirit.

But if I wanted to go further? Yes, I may know the strategy and the energy I am to use, but I'm still not too sure how to apply these things. I would then seek higher guidance. I would journey to the Sky Kingdom. Here I request if a higher being could speak with me. The being who appears is just as important as the counsel given! I would also like to note that the advice given here can include what you have to release and not only be what you need to do. In a little while, I see a Sacred Ancestor. This Sacred Ancestor is the spirit of a clan mother. She advises me how to use the elements of spirit, fire, and water and to present myself as I am when I am interviewed. I am admonished that I must speak with my family before a new job begins because this will greatly impact the time I can spend with them and they will need to adjust emotionally. She tells me that my new bosses will be understanding if I explain to them what I need not only in my professional life but also in my personal life. I am to be a leader of compassion and demonstrate that I sincerely care for the people who are around me and who are working under me. The fact that it was a clan mother who graciously came to speak with me already showed me that I need to be thinking like one. A clan mother is a tribal matriarch. She has many responsibilities, and one of them is to ensure that everyone is doing their part for the tribe so that things run smoothly.

Upon my return, I sit with all that I have been given. I start my practice by honoring and integrating the elements of fire, water, and spirit. I begin to use my Medicine tools and chants to welcome my kin, the Cougar, Rabbit, and Beaver, so they may stay connected with me from the realm of spirit to this physical world as I begin my job hunt. I also sit and ponder what the Sacred Ancestor told me about what it means to be a leader. I begin thoughtful discussions with my family about how this would impact them and ask their input.

As you can see, throughout this entire process I have combined what I have been given from the realm of spirit with my intellect. From what I received, I now know what tone my résumé should have and how to present myself when I go for an interview. With the insights that I have been given, I can recognize what type of company, work culture, and bosses to look for. I can now begin to verbalize what I can offer to a company. Since I had discussions with and feedback from my family, I can set healthy limits to preserve my home life before agreeing to take on responsibilities at the new job.

Walking between the worlds is not only a process of Balance, but it is also a wonderful way to cocreate with All Your Relations!

If you are like me, life never runs on only one question at a time. It is usually a flurry of activities and a multitude of questions that are circling me like hungry honeybees around sweet flowers. It can be very difficult for your Guardians to keep up with you! In the beginning, especially when you ask a question of them, there can be a delay. It is very much like communicating with someone on the moon. How confusing it is if you ask a question and then, in your rush and distraction, ask ten more. Finally, you slow down at the end of the week and your Guardian has their first chance to relay a message to you. You recognize that it is an answer of some sort, but because there has been such a delay in receiving the answer, you have no idea what it relates to! This is frustrating for you and for the ones who want to help you.

Example Two: Building a Relationship

Here is another common situation. Say that you meet someone and wish to be friends with them, or perhaps more. You talked to them enough to know that this individual is sane and safe. They are also interesting enough that you would like to pursue this, but you are not too sure what to do. The first step would be formulating the question: How do you pursue this relationship? Analyzing it, you realize that you would be willing to risk it.

The next step is establishing what your desired outcome is. The optimal result is that this becomes a healthy and happy romantic relationship, but you are willing to settle for companionship or good friendship.

Step number three is to consider if the desired outcome is in Balance. Why or why not? When you check within your own Heart and speak with your Guardians, it does not really matter one way or the other. This particular event has no karmic impact nor major influence on your life path. In essence, this relationship could enrich your life but does not have the power to strongly throw your life out of Balance, though it will definitely impact your emotions.

Step four is to find what strategies you will use in approaching this person and situation by visiting your kin. Your journey takes you to the Lower Kingdom. Here you are visited by a beautiful Horse that matches the energy of the person you are trying to become close to. The Horse, although wild, is calm and friendly in your presence. Your personal Power Animals bring you apples and ask you to sit and wait. They place one of the apples between you and the Horse. The Horse comes toward you in his own time. After eating the apple, he does not shy when you start petting him upon the neck. Then he starts to toss his head playfully and invites you to run in the fields with him, but he does not let you ride him. You notice that overhead there are a couple of Crows that are friends of the Horse. These birds are laughing and singing and soon are joined by more Crows. Overall, it is a happy scene, and after a little while, your Guardians ask you to return to the Fire of Your Heart and back to the Middle Kingdom.

In this particular case, the spirit of the Horse represents the free and proud spirit of the person whom you are trying to connect with. The apple signifies that innocence and sweetness is the strategy to be used. Since your personal Power Animals told you to wait after they placed an apple between you and the Horse, this represents initiating the friendship but not trying to force anything. Bide your time! The Horse inviting you to run and play in the fields symbolizes a successful outcome at least for the beginning of a wonderful friendship. The friends of the Horse, the Crows that are laughing and singing overhead, let you know that your potential friend is gregarious. Be prepared to socialize.

Step five is finding out which of the elements are most needed so you know which energy to apply. Here you focus and call to Heart and mind the energy of the Horse that you had come across in the Realm of Deeper Earth. Honor and connect with each of the elements one by one. The elements that are the strongest are the ones that should be engaged. Say in this particular case that the elements that came out the strongest were earth and air. When you connect with earth, you receive the image of many beautiful things. With the element of air, you hear and see a storyteller telling an entertaining teaching story. In this case, the element of earth lets you know that this person appreciates gifts and enjoys experiences that are physical. The element of air lets you know that this person also enjoys good conversations and likes entertaining stories.

Step six is requesting higher guidance to understand the overall picture of the situation at hand. You choose to journey to the Sky Kingdom because you are nervous and want confirmation that what you are thinking is correct. Here you are met and greeted by a god who is known as the Lord of Transformation. He appears to you in this youthful form and informs you that although this might seem casual, you and the person in question will have a profound effect on each other. In order for this relationship to grow, you are advised to release expectations of how your relationships and attempted romantic relationships have ended in the past. He counsels you to be in the present moment and truly see the person who is in front of you and not compare them to someone of your past. He also counsels you that regardless of outcome, you will be richer from having had a friendship with this individual, and he gives you confirmation that it will not distract you from your life path or spiritual growth.

Step number seven is to sit with all the information that you have gathered. It helps you get it into perspective that although it is worth pursuing this relationship, you do not have to stake your Heart on it. This allows you to relax and enjoy the natural unfolding of this friendship, and now you know that you have to be the initiator but then to be patient and allow this person to respond in their time.

Take time to go through the steps that are needed. As you begin to grow in your practice and your relationships with the spirits of your guides and helpers, you will be able to streamline this process and perhaps even come up with your own methods. Although it is a seemingly long and slow procedure in the beginning, as you begin to better interpret what is being shared with you and know where to journey to find what you need, you will see that this process can go very quickly. At times when you are frustrated or impatient, it might be sorely tempting to use a shortcut. The result will be that your mind and Heart will begin to argue. Remember that on this Good Red Road, the Heart and head (which is your mind) need to work together like two horses that are in perfect step. This will help avoid confusion and you will feel a sense of security in the decisions that you make. This is because, as we would say, "all of you is in one place," which means you have responded to all aspects of your needs and thoughts satisfactorily.

Never forget that life is in flux! The information you receive is useful, but remember to pay attention to how situations can change. Adapt and act accordingly.

ELEVEN

Maintaining Your Connection in Daily Life

To Walk on a traditional Native American shamanic path is to keep strong your connection to the sacred both in this world and in the realm of spirit. It is not one of journeying only when you need something. Training to be a living bridge between the worlds is not simply a set of skills that you practice sporadically. It is a way of being that defines how you will move through your life. This requires careful cultivation on a daily basis. Let me describe the different ways.

Self with the Great Spirit

It is said that all things come from the Creator and all things go back to the Creator. It is the Breath of the One that moves us all. Take time every day to give thanks for your life and the gift of free will. It is customary to give these prayers of thankfulness upon rising and retiring for the day. Some tribal practices are offering smudge with prayer, singing a traditional song, drumming, or playing the flute. The benefit of doing this is that it prevents you from focusing only on the negative things that may be happening in your life or around you. It keeps the perspective that the blessings are always there if you but reach for them. I ask for you to make it a practice to focus on four things that you are grateful for every day. I recommend reflecting on two of them upon rising and two of them before retiring for the day. This is a much better use of your time than surfing mindlessly on the internet or switching from one TV channel to the next because you are bored.

Take time to sit still and connect with your own Heart at least once a day. In this sacred place within you is where the Creator dwells. Your Heart is a place of peace where you can center yourself no matter where you are. When you are here, you can release whatever pain or sorrows have been burdening you. Allow yourself to feel the fire of life and know that you are loved by the Great Spirit because you are part of the Medicine Wheel of life. The benefit of this practice is that you will be able to feel subtle messages regardless of where they come from because you will be accustomed to listening with your Heart.

Let me share with you a practice that I like to do daily. In Native American spiritual tradition, simplicity is a value. Every day I focus on a blessing that I would like for myself and for the world. Say, for example, that I choose love. I meditate on what divine love means. I envision it as a color, usually pink. Then I feel the energy of it within my Heart. With every heartbeat, I allow this energy to fill every fiber of my being. As I inhale, I receive love, and as I exhale, I send the love that is in my Heart back out into the world and as a gift to the Creator. I then consciously do my best to embody divine love as I go through my day. In order to get the maximum benefit of this exercise, choose a different word every day and explore various expressions of it.

Self with Sacred Self

As you have learned, journeying is done both in this world and the spirit world, and because of this, taking care of yourself and connecting with your sacred self will be key to keeping your health and strength upon this path. At this time, I would like to reiterate that maintaining your body by eating well, getting enough rest, and getting proper exercise is showing respect to yourself by preserving the vehicle that houses your soul. Sustaining yourself should not be a drudgery. Take time to discover what you enjoy that also reinforces your health and your overall well-being. This means doing things that help you release and relieve stress as you go about your everyday routines. This will help you in your shamanic practice because you will have the vitality you need for journeying, and your mind will be receptive to messages from the spirits and All Your Relations because it will not be preoccupied and restless.

In the native teachings, the environment is an extension of our bodies. It would be counterproductive to take excellent care of yourself while being in a personal space that is dirty or toxic. Keep your place clean and uncluttered. Let your home hold things that give you joy and are a reflection of who you are now. Just as clear air is healthy for your lungs, a tidy space generates clean energy that supports your spirit body. I also recommend creating a space, no matter how small, in your home for your sacred practices. It is good to have a sanctuary for yourself. It will give you the comfort of knowing you have a place of serenity that you can count on. From a shamanic standpoint, this special space will be conducive to going into the Dreamtime and will be a spiritual workshop. Since it will be strictly attuned to these energies, it will also be easier to receive messages from your Guardian and helpers.

Let me give you an idea of what a personal sanctuary might look like. It would be in a quiet spot in your home and preferably painted in your favorite soothing color. It would have a comfortable place to sit and no electronics other than the technology you use to listen to drumming or peaceful music conducive to journeying and spiritual work. There would be different items honoring your personal Medicines. I will describe what some of these items could be a little further on. The space should also have a table or piece of furniture that can hold your items for smudging and other sacred tools. Ideally, this is a space where you have the option to dim the lights or safely use a candle if you require softer lighting for journeying or meditating. The only people who should be allowed to enter are those who have your explicit permission and who truly understand that they are going into your personal sacred sanctuary.

Self with Personal Medicines

Your personal Medicines are an extension of your sacred self. This includes your Guardian Spirit, your personal Power Animals, and all sacred and divine beings that are assisting you in your journey. As I mentioned previously, placing items that represent them in your sacred space is not worshiping them but is a way to strengthen your bond with Medicines. These items also make it easier for them to connect with you. As these objects are sacred, they should be stored in your sanctuary or at the very least in a place that is out of the way so no one touches them without your permission. Which, quite frankly, should be hardly ever if at all.

Objects that are chosen to represent your personal Medicines can be practically anything at all. They can be stones, pictures, small statues, or even a fabric, like a tapestry, that has certain images of the being that you wish to honor. The important part is that whenever you see or touch this sacred object, it helps you make an instant connection with your Medicine. In truth, these items act as a conduit so that divine energy channels from the Dreamtime into this Middle Kingdom.

Studying and researching are key to developing a deeper intellectual understanding of what these sacred beings are all about. It will help you connect with your Medicines in a more meaningful way if your mind can follow what your Heart already knows. The effort that you put into your studies and practices will demonstrate to your helpers that you genuinely care to learn about them and want to grow a deeper relationship with them. There are many places to get information, but you must discern which ones are accurate and true. Books, reference materials, and websites can only go so far. I encourage you to seek out teachers and elders that are respected and recognized for the knowledge that they keep. This means looking up and respectfully asking questions about the backgrounds of these potential mentors by asking who their teachers were and how they came to hold the lessons that they share. Working with a teacher who has experience with your type of Medicine will make things so much easier than trying to figure it out all on your own. In person, an elder can show you nuances that would be lost in translation in any other medium. Properly living what you are taught also ensures that in some way the ancient traditions and teachings carry on into the future. I do not want to discourage you from learning on your own. In truth, it takes both forms of study, by yourself and under a skilled teacher, to fully develop your shamanic gifts.

Objects may hold the energy of your spirit helpers, but they are only physical representations. You must interact with what they represent and practice what they are trying to teach you. Strive to embody the essence of your Medicines. In this manner, you are honoring them spiritually. Doing this also has the benefit of you more easily being able to identify and channel their energies smoothly when you are performing your shamanic practices. Do your best to incorporate the different lessons and advice as they are given to you. Do not follow blindly what is said to you. Remember, this is meant to be a lifelong, ongoing conversation. Here your questions are always welcome, and the insights and answers presented to you by your teachers seen and unseen are reasonable, enrich your life and the lives of others, and make sense from a bigger perspective.

As I mentioned in an earlier section of this book, when I first started as a young apprentice, one of the first Medicines that came to me was the Wolf. Back then, there were no books written on the topic and the internet did not exist, so I had little success researching what spiritual meaning or lessons this personal Power Animal held. Although I did study from a biological standpoint the survival strategies and social structure of this animal, it still was not clear how this pertained to me as a human being and for my shamanic development. It was my Medicine Teachers at the time from both the Iroquois Nation and Seneca Nation who taught me the spiritual elements of this sacred animal. It was these elders who showed me how this related to me as an individual and how this was relevant to our community. I am grateful that they showed me the different prayers and rituals that allowed me to fully embody—or as we would call it, Walk—with this Medicine in the sacred way. Under the guidance of my Medicine Teachers, I ritualistically journeyed with the spirit of the Wolf. My first drum was created shortly after that. I could feel the Power of the Wolf just by holding it! Every time I used it to journey, it reinforced my bond with my personal Medicine. Each time I drummed, I would remember the lessons of this sacred animal. This is one of the ways I was made to honor the Wolf.

Not all Power Animals are serious, and embodying their Medicine to honor them can be very enjoyable depending on who it is. River otters are fun-loving animals. You can tell they truly get great pleasure just from gliding in the water and being with each other. They are very affectionate and even hold paws when they are snoozing on the river so as not to lose each other. You might find that you like water and playing in the water because it is therapeutic for you. You could literally learn to play games and introduce humor and lightness of being to various situations and into your routines. Showing more signs of affection to your family and close friends is another way you could mirror the behavior of this particular Power Animal. All these activities would be an excellent way to Walk with and honor this Medicine.

This goes far beyond your personal Power Animals! The same process should be followed when learning to work with Sky Beings. One can read up on Lord Feathered Serpent, White Buffalo Calf Woman, Lady Sekhmet, an archangel, or any other divine being, but you will find that the relationship will be much richer only through interacting and journeying with Them on a consistent basis.

This is a very basic ritual that you can use to turn one of your items into a sacred object: You can ask for one of your objects to be empowered by one of your Guardians. After studying and researching that specific sacred being, journey into the Fire of Your Heart with that Guardian while holding on to the object that is meant to honor them. Ask the spirit to fill that item with their Power so that it becomes Medicine. Realize, however, that this will only work for your personal items. To make Medicine for others takes years of study and careful practice under the supervision of a teacher.

Self with All Your Relations

Native American cultures, like most indigenous cultures around the world, have a tribal mindset. It is impossible to only think about the individual without also thinking of the impact on the whole. I agree with the thought that what we do to the earth we do to ourselves and would extend that thought by saying that what we do to ourselves we also do to the earth. Here is a simple example of what I am talking about: Around the world, thousands of people put on sunblock in order to avoid sunburn and skin cancer. However, since the vast majority of people are not aware that these lotions are not friendly to our oceans, they are accidentally poisoning the sea. In turn, the sea life swims in these unclean waters and ingests these unnatural chemicals. Completing the circle, the waves of the ocean become toxic as well as the fish we harvest for food, and in the end, we poison ourselves too.

Walking on the Good Red Road as a shaman means setting an example for others by mindfully stepping as gently as you possibly can upon Earth Mother. "Living green" is not a modern concept. It has been a way of life for centuries for indigenous people around the world. Embrace this teaching that says that the earth does not belong to us but to the generations yet to be born. This means not only the human children but also the off-spring of *All* Our Relations! Living ecologically is one way that you can strengthen your connection to nature in this century. You will also be preserving your Medicines and your kin. It is honoring the Sacred Hoop of Life, which is one of the fundamental lessons on this path.

Never take more than you can give, and always be mindful of closing the circle. As much as you are able, when you buy things, pay attention to how they will be disposed of at the end of their use. Try always to purchase food items from sources that are responsibly sustained and harvested. Give back to the earth by planting trees. It does not have to be complicated. It could be as simple as picking up trash you see as you walk along the shore-line of the beach or strolling through a park. These simple acts of kindness to Earth Mother and All Your Relations will earn you love and trust from the Ancestors of the Land and Waters. You will find that as you Walk with love and respect upon the earth, the animals, the plants, the stones, the waters, the trees, the skies—indeed, *all* things—will wish to communicate with you and assist you on your life's journey. I personally cannot count all the times when my life has been so difficult that I have needed to go out for a walk completely preoccupied with my thoughts and had All My Relations reach out to guide and heal me. You will find this will be true for you too. You could go for a simple stroll expecting nothing at all and feel the embrace of the breath of the trees and the energy of joy from the birds.

A best friend of mine one time wondered if this was just co-incidence or if this was for real. She is a very amazing and kind person and had been studying with me on and off throughout the years while learning to Walk on this traditional shamanic path. I will never forget the bright, sunny winter day when we were on a cruise with some of our very good friends and we docked at a port. We all decided to go on a self-guided tour to the island's botanical gardens. We were all having fun and laugh-ing as we were talking about nothing at all, as friends will do. At one point, we saw a blur darting through the air. We stopped to see what it was. It turned out to be a hummingbird! The hum-mingbird stopped in front of my best friend. She laughed and looked up at it. The rest of us did as well, thinking that the bird was only curious and would soon take off. But every time my best friend moved or changed her position within the group, the little bird consistently stayed squarely in front of her face. It was only after she acknowledged the feeling of joy in embracing life that the hummingbird was trying to convey to her that it nod-ded its little beak at her as if in salute and then buzzed away in a flash.

At that point in her life, she was asking the Great Spirit and All Her Relations to show her what she needed to focus on to improve her life. This tiny messenger came to her because she Walks so consciously upon the earth and cares for nature. And so it is that we will go out for stroll, and it is no longer an uncommon thing (but it is still quite remarkable) for different animals to come up to one of us, wait to be acknowledged, and make sure that the message has reached our Hearts so that we know what it relates to before going back out into their homes in the wild. Remember that Our Relatives are wild and will act true to their natures, so always respect them by keeping a healthy distance and observing them only from afar!

Go with love and respect for nature and wild creatures, and this will be returned to you many times over, more than you can ever expect. You will find at moments of greatest need that because you have taken the care to live mindfully and lovingly, the beings of nature will reach out to assist you in any way that they can. This is not limited to the realm of the energetic and spiritual. It could be as simple as because you have helped preserve some of the rain forest, a life-giving, lifesaving herb was preserved, which in turn might in the future save your life or the life of someone you know. We are all connected on the Medicine Wheel of life.

I would teach you the ways of the peaceful shaman. As a living bridge between the worlds, Walking as a traditional shaman means that in addition to being ecologically minded, you move mindfully and with compassion among people. This is not to say that you will never get angry or frustrated at the things that people do. This would be unrealistic and foolish! However, simple acts of kindness or a smile may relieve the tension in the people around you. This in turn helps lessen the toxicity and negativity that exists so prevalently in our stressful world to-day. Although it may not be easy to live in this way, doing good for goodness's sake while honoring your own needs has been a sacred teaching in many cultures throughout the centuries. As you do these things, you will discover that divine beings, sacred beings, and Spirits of the Earth will notice. As you continue to go forward in this practice, you will find that they will more eas-ily listen to you and guide you, for they will see you as a person who has an open and pure Heart.

You are demonstrating that you are capable of patience with a potential to comprehend more profound concepts with your entire being instead of just with your mind. All too many times, people are only receptive to what they want and do not take the time to fully understand the advice and Power these divine spirits are gifting them. Life, it is said, is nothing but a reflection. When following these exercises becomes more than merely a practice to develop your gifts, reach a specific goal, and grow into a way of being, you will notice that good things are hap-pening to you that you did not expect, such as honest strangers offering kindness to you in troubled times. You will find that life will become more beautiful as it grows in spiritual grace, and your connections to the sacred become more profound despite all its hardships.

When living in harmony is the norm, then the causes of imbalances and strife will be more obvious. In turn, as a tra-ditional shaman, understanding what can create harmony and discord will assist you in knowing what to do and what to say so that you can be the most use to others in their growth and in building a better community. In my tradition, it is said that the shaman is initiated twice, once by the spirits and once by the community that they will serve. What good will it do to talk to all beings in the universe if your people do not trust you and reject the help you can bring them? Conversely, what good is it if everyone loves you but the sacred beings seen and unseen refuse to listen to you or offer you their assistance? As you can see, it is of vital importance to cultivate good relationships in this world and in all others as you journey between them.

Conclusion

As you have found out, there are different levels of journeying between the worlds. The more you speak to your Guardians on a continual basis and are open to the subtle energies and spirits around you (after they are screened by your Protectors as safe to approach, of course), the more you will find that all you need to do is be in a contemplative state in order to receive advice and sense the type and intensity of Power that is in your surroundings. If you ask questions, remember to use points of reference so that you recall which question a message is trying to answer. As you practice focusing on and directing sacred energy from your Waterfall to open your Heart more deeply, you will be able to easily channel the Medicine from your helpers into what you are doing. When you are in this receptive state and when you are able to sustain it, you will be in the perfect mode to remain connected to spiritual Power while crafting sacred and ritual items. It is in this state that you would "breathe life" into a ritual item. Drumming, chanting, and dancing help you connect with your Power more quickly before journeying. These practices bond you more concretely with your personal Medicine and greatly enhance it. It takes time to develop stamina. When your body asks for a break, take one right away to avoid physical exhaustion and spiritual burnout.

As you become completely immersed in the Breath of the Creator, this is when you can do your most profound journeying and be able to shape-shift into other forms, such as animals on the spirit side. Pacing yourself and becoming attuned to each kingdom's vibrational rate is how you achieve a greater capacity to journey much further in and between the worlds.

I know that I have only scratched the surface of this ancient tradition with you. I hope I have inspired you and that you will continue to practice. May what I shared with you enrich your life and in turn bring more good Medicine into the worlds. Until we meet again, my friend, may the Great Spirit bless you and All Our Relations watch over you. *Wanishi.* Thank you.

Dah-neh Ho! It is finished!

Resources

I welcome you to share time with me again by reading my writing or training with me directly. Please go to my website to sign up for my newsletter and check to see my latest events and news at www.eagleskyfire.com.

I have posted traditional chants and their teachings on my website if you would like to purchase them to help you in your shamanic practice. I have a free audio that you can use as well. To support your journeying, it is very useful if the music or drumbeat includes a signal for when it is time for you to return.

Many of my services are available virtually or by phone for your convenience. Sign up for my newsletter to learn about the latest classes, workshops, and events in addition to reading my blogs such as *Flow of the River,* which talks about how this sacred energy will be influencing us every week.

A few of the topics that I mentor on include intuitive development, past-life work, shamanism, communicating with your Spirit Guardian, soul work, Native American spirituality, and meditation. If there is an area that you would like to be mentored in, please contact me.

I also do private readings and have helped many people around the world. I offer the readings of spirit, earth, and harmony. Please visit my website for explanations of what each type of reading can provide you, and you can schedule your appointment by contacting me directly or by going to my website's calendar. I welcome you to contact me through my website at eagleskyfire.com/contact or by instant messaging me on Facebook.

To Write to the Author

If you wish to contact the author or would like more information about this book, please write to the author in care of Llewellyn Worldwide Ltd. and we will forward your request. Both the author and the publisher appreciate hearing from you and learning of your enjoyment of this book and how it has helped you. Llewellyn Worldwide Ltd. cannot guarantee that every letter written to the author can be answered, but all will be forwarded. Please write to:

Eagle Skyfire
℅ Llewellyn Worldwide
2143 Wooddale Drive
Woodbury, MN 55125-2989

Please enclose a self-addressed stamped envelope for reply,
or $1.00 to cover costs. If outside the U.S.A., enclose
an international postal reply coupon.

Many of Llewellyn's authors have websites with additional information and resources. For more information, please visit our website at http://www.llewellyn.com.

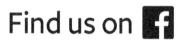